GETTING

THE MEDIA

A guide to the film, broadcasting,
video and publishing industries

SECOND EDITION

Emma Caprez

TROTMAN

This second edition published in 1998 in Great Britain by
Trotman and Company Limited, 12 Hill Rise, Richmond,
Surrey TW10 6UA
First edition published by Trotman in 1995

© Trotman and Company Limited 1998

British Library Cataloguing in Publication Data
A catalogue for this book is available from the British Library

ISBN 0 85660 384 8

Printed and bound in Great Britain
by Creative Print and Design (Wales) Ltd

CONTENTS

ABOUT THE AUTHOR

Emma Caprez studied for her BA in Design and Media Management at Thames Valley University. For her final year project she researched, wrote and illustrated a book on the history of the Ealing School of Art. She graduated with First Class Honours in 1993. She has worked on other research projects including one on the feasibility of dramatherapy for people with disabilities for the First Chance Project. She has written several children's books as well as writing for two international music papers *Rumba* and the *LA Rock Review*. She has also contributed towards university literature.

ACKNOWLEDGEMENTS

Thanks to the Contributors:

Narinder Banwait – Zenith Media
Dinah Caine and Kate O'Connor – Skillset
Teresa Cross – Flying Fish Video Production Company
Sue Davis – ITV Network Centre
Paul 'Chip' Gardner – Big Breakfast
Colin Hambrook – DAIL (Disability Arts In London)
Julian Hanshaw – National Film and Television School
Jamie Payne – Panico Media Workshop
Joy Peraud – Greenford and Northolt Gazette
Maggie Sanson – FT2
Lucy Wade – BBC Radio 5 Live
Katrina Wray – IPC Magazines
Anne Fenton – Moving Image Society – BKSTS
Celine Cava – Barefoot Books
Shay Leonard – Freelancer
Spencer MacDonald – BECTU

Thanks for their support:

The West London TEC, Tim Harrison, Skillset, Andrew Ward, David
Grant, Seth Brown, John Gummery, Coral Schubert, Andy Atherton
from Abbey Road Interactive, Mr Knuckey and Mr Edwards from
Heston Community School and 6th form students, Angela McRobbie,
Bernadette Wyatt and Majella, the School of European,
International and Social Studies , students at Thames Valley
University, Maisie Kazen and Morfydd Jones and Liz Murray at
Trotman

A big thank you to Narinder Banwait who helped research
the information for this book, Peach Kazen for additional Directory
research and Richard Pool for the loan of his office.

Special thanks to Rook Randle, Biba Maya, Suky Ella and
Arlette Caprez.

FOREWORD

The media industry is a fast expanding sector in London and offers unlimited scope for people to pursue a wide range of interesting careers and occupations. For these reasons, the West London Training and Enterprise Council is committed to a series of initiatives supporting and promoting the Industry.

The competition for jobs in this sector is fierce. We hope this guide will help you succeed in one of the most exciting activities in Britain.

Dr Phil Blackburn
Chief Executive, West London Training and Enterprise Council

PREFACE

Dreams, delusions and tears. To achieve a dream career in 'the media' you need to strip away delusions. This book gives you good advice – advice from those who have gained a first foothold within the media industries.

If you think a degree is going to open doors – forget it. It may help, but it certainly won't be the answer, not even a Media Studies degree. Work from the premise that NVQs may become a professionally recognised qualification. Recognise the reality that contacts and networking are crucial. Work from the premise that luck, tenacity, more luck, rethinking, and yet more luck are vital.

If you are looking for work in the media, be prepared to start at the bottom, be badly paid, work 16-hour days and be engaged on short-term contracts. If you are prepared for all this, this book will help you to be one step ahead of the competition.

In part you will achieve this by making things happen. Ensure that if you are taking a diploma or degree there is sufficient freedom to gain work experience whenever you can get it. Ensure that you think flexibly and that transferable skills, and multiskilling are saleable commodities. Above all, be tenacious. When you get told time and time again, 'No', don't give in, keep trying. One day your tears will turn to your dream.

Dr David Grant,
Associate Dean for Special Needs
at Thames Valley University

INTRODUCTION TO THE SECOND EDITION

According to a recent Mori Poll, 49% of graduates are interested in a career in journalism or broadcasting.

This book examines the avenues open to those people interested in following a career in film, broadcasting (television and radio), video and publishing. What you are about to read is meant to give you a realistic and responsible account of these industries as they are today, including the fierce competition, the need to 'multiskill', and the increase in freelance work. Those who are seriously determined to achieve a career in the media will not be put off, but may become more aware and knowledgeable of what has to be one of the most competitive industries of modern times.

☐ THE MEDIA

The industries described in this book have been referred to as 'the media'. Although the publishing industry is obviously different from the broadcasting one, many of the entry methods are similar, so while those differences are appreciated – and often pointed out – the collective term of 'the media' has been used where appropriate.

Changes in the past decade

The 1990 Broadcasting Act – which requires the BBC and Channel 3 network to commission a quarter of its schedule from outside organisations – saw a massive growth in the independent production sector, although only a very small minority of these production companies actually secure the commissions for television broadcast. This Act has put the BBC and Channel 3 network into a more competitive economic climate, which has also had a knock-on effect in regard to issues such as staff numbers and training. The BBC and Channel 3 network must also now compete for commissions with television publishers Channel 4, which was launched in the early

1

1980s, and Channel 5, which went on air in 1997. Added to this are the dramatic changes that have affected the broadcasting, film and video industries over the past decade.

Along with the advent of satellite and cable companies, market growth, the restructuring of many important organisations, and the changing role of the trade unions, there has been a shift from permanent to freelance contracts. Technological development has meant the application of computers to many jobs in the industry.

Fierce competition

Competition in the film, broadcasting, video and publishing industries is fierce, and each year there are a greater number of young people who want to make a career in the media. The level of practical training is generally an important consideration to the industry's employers, as is work experience. However, just because you are prepared to work for a company for free to gain some experience, doesn't mean that placements will be easy to find. Thousands of people are looking for work experience, and the supply doesn't always meet the high level of demand.

Those who survive in the media not only know how to use their own initiative, but are very persistent in their quest to gain a place in this highly competitive industry. You really do need to have a passion for the area of work you have chosen to build a career in, because it will generally involve sacrifices in your private life.

'You may work 12-hour shifts starting early in the morning, at weekends or maybe away in uncomfortable surroundings. Competition means that you need to be available for as long as it takes. This can prevent people who are parents developing careers.'
Employee in Broadcasting

Start young

It is best to start young if you want to follow a media career. After training, and especially if you go on to do a postgraduate degree, you will eventually have to look for a job. If you were a mature student you would still probably start off in a job on the bottom rung of the ladder. There you would be in competition with much younger people who are often better able to cope on the low salaries which these entry level jobs generally offer, for example Sales (Television and

Radio air-time), Administration and Secretarial, Technical Assistant Traineeships, Videotape/Film Editor Traineeships, Assistant Floor Managers, Runners and Journalist/Subeditor Traineeships. The type of wages these jobs can offer – probably anything from £8000 to £14,000 per annum – may be impossible for a more mature person, especially one with dependants, to survive on.

Freelance employment

According to a survey conducted by Skillset, the industry training organisation for film, broadcasting and video, there are now 54% freelancers within the specialised labour force of these particular industries. New entrants are also more likely to be freelance, with 70% of people who entered the industry since 1990 being freelance straightaway. The Skillset survey, which had a 40% response rate, also showed that freelancers work an average of 173 days a year.

Unlike those on contracts of at least a year (generally core staff, producers, presenters and researchers), or the permanent staff (managers, administrators and essential professional technicians), freelancers are employed only when and if they are needed. The increasing trend towards freelance employment has also meant a greater insecurity in the industry. Added to this, approximately half of all freelancers earn less than £20,000 per annum – half of whom earn £12,000 or less.

In the publishing industry, too, many of the jobs such as copyediting, proofreading and design are carried out by freelancers.

Two-thirds of freelancers are based in London and the South East and, for this reason, most of the following information is based on what is happening, and what is available, in the Greater London area.

Computer literacy

The 1990s have seen massive strides forward in the use of technology, and the media industry is no exception. Computers are now used at every stage of the production process, so its vital to be computer literate if you are pursuing a media career. News pages, for example, are made up electronically on screen so Subeditors must be experienced at desktop publishing (DPT). Computers are used in areas such as animation, designing book covers and editing films, programmes and videos to name but a few.

The 1990s have also seen a rapid convergence of media, computing and communications technologies. Reporters may write their stories on laptop computers out on a job and send the copy, via a telephone line by means of e-mail, to the newspaper in seconds. Photographs can also be sent in this way, and virtually all published photos you see today will have been manipulated in some way to produce the perfect image by the aid of a computer.

The digital age

The digital age is upon us, bringing with it better quality in both sound and vision. (July 1998 is the target set for launching digital terrestrial television. BBC Radio has been broadcast digitally since September 1995 and commercial digital radio is due to come on air sometime in 1999.) The signals are more compressed than in the existing analogue techniques, increasing space for a greater choice of television and radio channels. Widescreen and flatscreen televisions will eventually become more affordable and more people will have the opportunity to access television pictures through their computers and plan programmes to their own agendas via telephone connected systems.

The digital age has also opened up new possibilities in multimedia. Multimedia is a multimillion pound business and opens up yet another avenue for those seeking a career in media. The Internet, which allows anyone with a computer modem and a telephone line to reach a worldwide audience, has been claimed by some to be as revolutionising now as when printing was invented. It is sure to play an increasingly important part in the communication of the global village through the development of multimedia. At the beginning of 1998 we witnessed for the first time on BBC's *Tomorrow's World*, a live jam between musicians from around the world via the information super-highway. As technologies develop possibilities abound.

Technological development

The development in technology has, to some degree, also had a negative effect on new entrants joining the film, broadcasting and video industries. For example, the introduction of 'non-linear' editing – where the post-production process is performed entirely on computer – is, some say, quicker, cheaper and more creative. However, while diminishing the mess on the cutting room floor, it has also diminished the need for an Assistant Editor, which is an entry-level grade. As the Editors who have moved over to the non-linear method were the ones who trained on the old system, they had already gained the skills of visual literacy. If there is no longer a need for Assistant Editors, how will the non-linear editors of the future gain their visual literacy skills? This training will almost definitely have to be taught at universities and colleges.

Multiskilling

Keeping staff numbers down to a minimum has meant the introduction of 'multiskilling', where one person performs a range of tasks formerly done by different people. Multiskilling often means that people are required to work longer hours, not necessarily for more money, and possibly with less attention to quality. However, having a greater diversity of skills may mean employees enjoy their work more and are qualified for a greater variety of jobs, allowing for more movement across the industry. Originally, for example, staff either worked in television or radio, but now it is increasingly common to crossover and work in both (bimedia).

Training

A concern of the industry at large is that many of today's new entrants are not properly trained. There is currently less opportunity for training within the industry, such as the BBC and ITV, than there has previously been. Now new entrants are expected to gain their training independently, which can be very expensive, especially as they constantly need to retrain to keep up-to-date with technology, and keep themselves in the market for career advancement.

NVQs

Skillset has been involved with the introduction and implementation of the different specialised broadcast, film and video NVQs (National Vocational Qualifications) which are awarded when a person has gained the required competence standard to do a specific job. NVQs in Print Journalism and Stills Photography are already in place, and may be the way, in future, that employers identify if a person is qualified to do the job. This should prevent employers taking on people who are not properly trained. (See page 46 for more information.)

The media industry is tough to get into and, once you have your foot in the door, it can be very hard and unglamorous work. But year on year, more and more people make it their career goal, and every year new people **do** enter the industry. Of course the media industry has a lot to offer. You will work with some highly motivated and creative people, and the camaraderie of teamwork is a big plus. Personal, intellectual and creative satisfaction, and the pleasures associated with this industry, make it a very satisfying career choice. With the right training, work experience and determination, you may just make it!

SKILLS AND PERSONAL ATTRIBUTES

Although the film, television, radio and publishing industries are all different and require a variety of skills and qualities depending on the nature of the job, these industries also have much in common. Look at the list below and assess if you have the relevant attributes for a job in the media.

- Communication skills
- Initiative
- Confidence
- Enthusiasm and tenacity
- Reliability and commitment
- Knowledge of the industry and what is going on
- Ability to work well (and safely) under pressure
- Ability to meet deadlines
- Ability to solve problems and think laterally
- Willingness to work long hours – stamina
- Computer literacy
- Willingness to develop new skills

Additional attributes you will require for journalism are:

- Good command of the English language, or the language you will be writing
- Keen interest in current affairs
- Interest in people, places and events
- Inquiring and critical mind
- News instinct
- Short-hand and typing skills
- Ability to write in an objective and concise style which is easy to understand
- Ability to sift the relevant facts from the irrelevant

Additional attributes you will require for book publishing are:

- Good command of the English language, or the language you will be writing

- Good spelling, grammar and punctuation
- Inquiring and critical mind
- Ability to sift the relevant facts from the irrelevant
- Commercial sense
- Time management/scheduling
- Attention to detail
- Concentration
- Good people skills

Most importantly of all, you will need to be able to establish good working relationships, as working in a team and networking are of paramount importance in the media industry, where obtaining freelance work is often through word of mouth. You may also require a full clean driving licence if travelling is part of your job. In addition, although there might not be any specific requirements for a degree in your chosen area of work, the majority of entrants are graduates. According to a recent Skillset survey 72% of freelancers had a degree, although not always in a media-related area. You will almost certainly need some kind of journalism training if this is the area of the media you have chosen to go into and a degree is almost a prerequisite for a career in book publishing.

☐ CONCLUSION

Work experience and qualifications can help you obtain work in whatever job area you wish to apply for and, as you can see from the lists above, it is not just the specialist skills you should emphasise to prospective employers. Transferable, business and personal skills, such as computer literacy, organisational ability and a good sense of humour, are often just as important. However, even if you have all the above attributes, these alone will not guarantee you a job. Luck – being in the right place at the right time and having useful contacts – still plays a major part in gaining employment. But be persistent...

Paul Gardener, Final Year Design and Media Management student with work experience on Channel 4's The Big Breakfast

Although Paul Gardner was still in his final year at Thames Valley University, he managed to find the time to gain as much valuable work experience as possible. His work experience as a runner has included work for Brian Lapping Associates (a production company) at the BBC and for Channel 4's *The Big Breakfast*.

'The first job at Brian Lapping was more interesting. I was phoning up, getting videotapes there on time, running errands for the producer and faxing, whereas on *The Big Breakfast* I was literally keeping the canteen stocked, but it was better because you were free to do what you wanted to. Once the job was done, you could walk out on to the set and take in what was going on… and as soon as you've been there a while you understand how live TV is put together and how quickly everyone has to work together as a team.'

Paul got his running job at *The Big Breakfast* on the strength of his CV, which he had recently redone: 'I redesigned it to make it more punchy and reduced it from three pages to one. I think it just landed on the desk at the right time. The girl who gave me the job said she pulled out the last 20 CVs that she wanted and said mine stood out, so they picked me!' Paul believes that the fact he had already gained some work experience, was doing a degree and wasn't too young – in his mid-twenties – helped him get the job.

The work, although they paid his expenses, was totally voluntary and began at 6am and finished at 2pm. Since then Paul has been offered additional paid trainee work with *The Big Breakfast*. Obviously how he behaved while gaining work experience there paid off.

'I learn quickly; I'm willing to take in everything. If somebody was showing me sound, then I'd pick up on it. I did a couple of hours cable-bashing for one day. I'd never done it before, I just volunteered for it. I wasn't afraid to volunteer for doing something and I was always keen on asking questions.'

Narinder Banwait, Publications Assistant at Zenith Media

Zenith Media is the buying arm of Saatchi and Saatchi and Bates advertising agencies. As Publications Assistant, Narinder looks at all the advertising agencies worldwide to find out how much money they are expected to spend on advertising in television, press (newspapers and magazines), cinema, radio and outdoor (posters) in the future. She is currently working on a book called *TV in Europe 2007*, which forecasts what the European countries will be spending on advertising up to the year 2007. The book costs £250. Narinder's job involves researching, writing and

9

desktop publishing at Zenith Media, and she has seen her name in print a lot since she began employment there.

After graduating with a 2:1 BA (Hons) in Design and Media Management from Thames Valley University, Narinder was employed as a Research Assistant at her university, helping to research the information for the first edition of *Getting into the Media.* She then travelled for a year before landing her job at Zenith Media. She originally applied for an Admin Assistant post and was told she had not got the job, but she had come second and that they would keep her details on file. Six months later she was called up as the Admin Assistant post had become available again. Her new boss told her that over 100 people had applied with her original application.

The reason she was selected was because her covering letter stood out. It was direct and to the point. 'I picked out the three main points in the job vacancy advert which said they were looking for someone well organised, who had computer skills and could do Word Perfect. I wrote about these in the covering letter and said I would love to find out more about the publishing industry. I was also told my CV stood out because it was one page, concise and showed I had a degree.' Narinder maintains that the type of degree she has – a BA in Design and Media Management – was irrelevant. 'What was important was that I had a

degree. In fact they often make jokes about media degrees in my office, so I have to tell them to watch it.' There are four other people working in Narinder's office and their degrees are in maths, Latin, history and science.

After two more months as Admin Assistant, one of the Publications Assistants left and Narinder was immediately offered the job. Her boss felt she was intelligent, hardworking and capable. She was not given a further interview.

Narinder did not always want to work in publishing. 'When I graduated I was pretty naive. I wanted to be a Camera Operator and aimed straight for the BBC, but I became disheartened after applying for four trainee posts, two of which were for people from ethnic minorities, and failed to even get short listed. I now want to progress in the magazine and newspaper industry and improve on my writing, layout and design skills.'

Any advice?
'I think it is important to decide the area of work you want to go into and then specialise in it when you are training. That way you really have something to offer when you leave college or university other than a little bit of knowledge of everything, which doesn't really help anyone. When you're at university it's up to you to get out of it what you need, so you really have to put the work in yourself.'

THE JOBS

There are numerous jobs in the media industry, and unless you have a knowledge of all of them, you won't know which one is really for you. Once you do know, it is important to find out as much as possible about the specific area of work you are interested in.

Do your research! You could do this by contacting people in the industry who are already doing the job you eventually want to do, and asking them for advice. Don't forget to ask the route they followed in order to get where they are today.

The personal attributes and skills listed under each job description are in addition to those highlighted in the previous chapter (page 7).

☐ TELEVISION, FILM AND VIDEO

Competition for entry into the television, film and video industry is fierce, and the digital age will not necessarily mean greater job opportunities since the new channels are likely to be offering a lot of repeats of what we have already viewed on other channels. That does not mean, however, there will not be opening for new recruits and here are the avenues which you should explore.

- Public sector television. BBC1 and BBC2 (national and regional)
- Channel 3 Network: Anglia TV, Border TV, Central Broadcasting, Carlton Communications, Channel TV, GMTV, Grampian TV, Granada TV, HTV, LWT, Meridian Broadcasting, Scottish TV, Tyne Tees TV, UTV, West Country TV, Yorkshire TV
- Channel 4, S4C (Sianel Pedwar Cymru)
- Channel 5
- Satellite and Cable TV
- Teletext
- The Internet
- Television, video and film production companies.
- Facility houses
- Film libraries

Job descriptions

Production Crew

Producer
Producers are the teamleaders of a production, responsible for hiring the crew and production team and making sure everything keeps within budget, goes to plan and meets the deadline. They are often involved with initiating ideas and responsible for raising the necessary finance. There are sometimes opportunities for trainee Assistants.
- Managerial skills
- Ability to recognise viable ideas
- Financial, business and management skills
- Experience of the industry
- Ability to motivate people and inspire ideas

Director
Directors must direct the actors, performers and technical staff to realise the creative interpretation of the treatment. They work closely with the Producer and liaise with the Editor in post-production. Sometimes the Director may also be the Producer.
- A strong visual sense
- Ability to motivate others
- Knowledge of technical equipment
- Relevant industry experience

Production Secretary/Manager
Work of the Production Secretary includes organising catering and transport, typing scripts and having responsibility for payments to freelancers etc.
- Organisational skills
- Administrative and financial skills
- Problem-solving ability

Production Assistant (PA)
More than just administrative and secretarial back-up, PAs liaise between the Producer, Director and the rest of the production team, observe script changes and continuity, book studios, and time the programme.
- Organisational skills
- Tact
- Secretarial and administrative skills
- Problem-solving ability

Writer

Writers are commissioned to write and edit scripts for production by television, film, video or radio, keeping to the guidelines laid down in the Producer's brief.
- Creativity
- Writing skills
- Ability to realise other people's ideas
- Ability to accept criticism
- Published work

Script Editor

Script Editors do more than just check scripts for accuracy, they look for new talent, initiate ideas, conduct research and rewrite scripts.
- Editorial skills
- Ability to spot potential
- Writing and research skills
- Experience of the industry

Researcher

The Researcher helps the Producer by finding necessary information as well as suggesting ideas. Researchers will make contacts, search out interviewees, and may help with script writing. They may be generalist or specialist (eg popular or factual programmes).
- Organisational skills
- Interviewing skills
- Tact
- Ability to work independently

Floor Manager (FM)

The FM mediates between the Producer and Director in the gallery and the studio floor, so must pass on instructions in a concise and tactful way. The FM is also responsible for the studio audience. There are sometimes trainee Assistant positions.
- Organisational skills
- Empathy
- Technical and safety experience
- Experience of industry

Presenter

The Presenter communicates directly to the viewer and consequently must look and sound the part to attract the target audience. Presenters must have the right personality to convey the image of the show. They may interview guests and write their own scripts.

Presenters have generally previously worked in the media, eg as a Researcher, Journalist or as a celebrity.
● Good voice and right image
● Charisma
● Experience of industry

Announcer
He or she makes announcements between programmes giving information on what programmes follow or if there is a transmission fault etc. They read from timed scripts which they may also write.
● Clear, friendly voice
● Ability to translate information well
● Ability to work independently

Runner
The runner is an all-round general assistant doing all the odd jobs from making tea to making deliveries. This is often the starting point for those entering the film, television and video industry. It is also a good opportunity to learn more about the area of the industry you wish to pursue.
● Sensitivity to pressurised colleagues
● Driving license an asset

Art/Design Department

Art Director
The Art Director realises the Director and Producer's vision by finding the necessary location and using set builders to adapt or create the setting both on location and in the studio.
● Good visual sense/knowledge
● Art training or theatrical experience
● Ability to make viable interpretations

Graphic Designer
Using the latest technology, Graphic Designers are able to generate highly creative on-screen graphics, title and credit sequences. The work is planned on a storyboard and must fit into the style of the production in addition to keeping to the required length. They will also be involved with any connected merchandise of a production.
● Creativity
● Good visual communication skills
● Ability to coordinate visuals with sound
● Graphic design training

Special Effects Designer

The Special Effects Designer must design, create and operate the special technical effects of a production so that they look believable. This can be anything from a fake bottle to explosions. Computers are increasingly used in this area.
- Ability to translate ideas
- Art or science training
- Good visual sense
- Relevant software knowledge
- Design experience

Animators

Animators use both drawn and computer-generated images and three-dimensional models to create the illusion of movement by film, video or special visual effects. These days animation can be incredibly high tech. The Animator may work from his or her own idea or be given work on a commission basis.
- Art school training
- Ability to work ideas within budget
- Relevant software knowledge

Director of Photography

The Director of Photography is responsible for ensuring each camera operator is interpreting visually what the Director is hoping to achieve. This means making decisions on the kind of lens and film to be employed.
- Technical interest in film and television
- Good visual sense
- Training and experience

Costume Designer

The Costume Designer will interpret from the script the costumes the Producer is hoping to achieve, taking into consideration historical accuracy and style. This requires researching the period the script is written in, working within budget and to a deadline. The Costume Designer must make, adapt or hire costumes.
- Creativity
- Financial awareness
- Training in fashion/theatre design
- Experience

Dressmaker

Personnel in this area work with the Costume Designer to make, adapt and alter costumes. They must be able to draw up patterns from sketches.

- Organisational skills
- Experience
- Pattern-cutting, tailoring and dressmaking skills

Dresser
The Dresser dresses the actors ensuring they are in the correct costumes and keeps the wardrobe stock in order.

- Attention to detail
- Organisational skills

Make-up Designer
Make-up and hairdressing maybe performed by one person or separately. The Make-up and Hairdressing Designer must interpret the requirements of the production and apply this to the actors, presenters or contributors. This requires research and expertise, especially when performing such tasks as making period wigs or applying a wound. The Make-up and Hairdressing Designer must ensure continuity throughout a production.

- Creativity
- Attention to detail
- Sensitivity
- Knowledge of history
- Training in make-up and hairdressing
- Portfolio of work

Props
Personnel who work in props must acquire, maintain and dress the set with properties or 'props' that are required in order to create the necessary look. They must also ensure continuity of a production.

- Attention to detail
- Good visual sense
- Research ability – knowing where to get the desired prop

Set Crafts
Personnel working in Set Crafts as identified by Skillset include: Construction Managers; Plasterers; Riggers/Scaffolders; Painters; Drapes; Carpenters; Woodcutters; Scene Hands; Scenic Operatives; Stage Hands; Workshop Storekeepers; Scenic Stores Assistants. They all work to the specifications of the Set Designer to portray, construct and maintain the scenery necessary to fulfil the production brief. This may also involve maintaining mechanical features.

- Safety awareness
- Attention to detail
- Specialist skills and training

Technical Crew

Camera Operator

The Camera Operator must record still and moving images by operating film or video cameras as instructed by the Director. Camera styles vary from the large studio camera to the lightweight digital video camera used for news items. Technological developments, particularly in digital technology, has enabled some camera operators to work independently. News journalists may now also operate their own camera.
- Knowledge of different camera types
- Technical skills and training
- Visual awareness

Sound Operator

The work of a Sound Operator involves recording, editing and dubbing sounds to production requirements.
- Good ear for sound quality
- Technical skills and training
- Experience

Lighting Director

The Lighting Director is responsible for creating the mood and tone of a production through lighting to meet the needs of the production. This is a planned operation and may be worked out on computer.
- Good visual sense
- Lighting design skills and experience

Engineer

Engineers are responsible for quality in Television and Radio transmission. They also maintain the equipment.
- Problem solvers
- Safety awareness
- Training in electronic, electrical, sound or mechanical engineering
- Experience

Clapper Loader

This is another area where newcomers may enter the industry. The Clapper Loader loads film in the cameras, notes film stock and

lenses used and identifies each take, either by snapping the clapper board or by using an electronic one.
- Ability to handle film stock
- Organisational skills

Vision Mixer (VM)
The VM operates a console which controls what's on screen. It integrates effects and switches from one camera to another and to pre-recorded inserts. The VM works to a timed script in live situations.
- Good concentration
- Instant reactions
- Creative and technical skills
- Experience

Editor
Either by using raw tape or, more likely, by computer (non-linear editing) the Editor cuts and pieces together the required sequences to the Director/Producer's brief.
- Relevant software training
- Visual literacy
- Attention to detail
- Technical training and experience

Further job functions

Marketing and Sales
Involved with raising of revenues, selling air time, negotiating sponsorship and coproduction rights, the Marketing and Sales team also develops merchandise such as toys and books.
- Marketing training and negotiating skills
- Experience

Press and Public Relations
Personnel in this department are responsible for informing the other media via press releases and promotional material about programmes, coming events and news.
- Writing skills
- Creativity

Archivist/Librarians
The personnel in this area provide collections of recorded, written, visual and sound material for use by production companies, etc.

- Knowledge of industry
- Accuracy
- Administrative skills
- Specialist training

Related television, film and video occupations
- Administration
- Broadcast support organisations
- Legal
- Information technology support
- Management
- Policy and planning
- Catering
- Finance
- Theatre
- Film processing labs
- Multimedia (see below)
- Radio (see below)
- Journalism (see below)
- Advertising (television and radio)

☐ RADIO

People looking for work in radio should investigate the following avenues:

- BBC Radio 1, 2, 3, 4 and 5 Live
- BBC local and regional radio
- BBC World Service – international
- Independent radio – national and local
- Independent radio production companies
- Community radio

Job descriptions

Please also refer to the Television, Film and Video section above as some job descriptions overlap, and also the Journalism section below.

Station Manager
The Station Manager must be knowledgeable about the target audience and make editorial decisions and policies about the content and style of the stations output to ensure their needs are met.

- Journalism and managerial skills
- Experience in radio industry

Studio Manager

The Studio Manager is responsible for booking and setting up studios for each programme. When on air the Studio Manager is also responsible for operating tape recorders, mixing between microphones, mixing in pre-recorded sound and ensuring the sound and feel of the programme are right. The Studio Manager may also edit previously recorded tapes.

- Organisational skills
- Technical skills
- Editing skills

Programme Producer

The Programme Producer must target their radio audience to attract as many listeners as possible by producing programmes they want to hear. Producers often initiate ideas for programmes, raise the necessary funds and make sure that the budget is adhered to. They manage the team to produce the programme and may also research and present it. Opportunities for trainees may exist.

- Creativity
- Negotiation skills
- Financial and business sense
- Editorial skills

Broadcast Assistant

So called because the Broadcast Assistant is often trained to work in both Radio and Television. The Broadcast Assistant generally assists the production team and work may include administration, research and developing ideas for programmes.

- Creativity
- Research and admin skills

Presenter/DJ

Presenters and DJs must sound right to meet the needs of the target audience. They may write and produce their own shows, which will include interviewing guests, cueing music and operating the sound desk in a live situation.

- Organisational skills
- Charisma and the right voice for the audience
- Technical skills
- Interviewing and Journalism skills or related media experience

Continuity Announcer
Personnel in this area must link together the programmes by providing the necessary information. They work to timed scripts which they often write themselves.
- A clear voice
- Good microphone technique
- Technical skills

Related radio occupations
- Finance and administration
- Engineering and technical support
- Promotions and publicity
- Management
- Marketing and sales
- Air traffic control
- Advertising (radio and television)
- Journalism (see section below)
- TV, film and video (see above)
- Broadcast support organisations

☐ JOURNALISM

Possible employers in the journalism sector are as follows:

- Newspapers – national, local, regional and ethnic
- Magazines and periodicals – consumer, business, professional or technical
- Broadcast: television and radio
- Internet
- News agencies
- Picture agencies and libraries
- Press support organisations
- Teletext
- Press and public relations
- Book publishing (see below)

Job descriptions

Editors
The Editor has complete autonomy but is also accountable in the case of complaints raised against the paper or magazine. The Editor decides what kind of readership to target. The Editor manages the

whole team, with regular meetings to discuss the stories being worked on and which direction they should take. They may also be responsible for allocating which reporter works on which stories.

- Managerial skills
- Editorial skills
- Legal and financial knowledge

News Producer/Editor
In broadcast journalism, the News Producer or Editor will be responsible for deciding the stories to be used, the angle to be taken on a particular news item and make decisions on how the final piece should be edited.

- Editorial skills
- Good visual sense

Subeditors
Subeditors are responsible for preparing news stories for press – thinking up headlines and subheadings, ensuring the language fits with the housestyle, that spelling and grammar are correct and that content is accurate. Subeditors cut the story to the required length and make sure it reads well. They may also lay out the pages on DTP systems. In Broadcast, the Subeditors may edit the news item.

- Creative
- Editorial skills
- Experience of the industry

Reporters
Personnel working in this area must find stories and write them up. Stories may be planned, eg a celebrity opening a local fete, or on the spot. While news items in national papers may be more 'exciting', all Journalists must work with people, events and places. Reporters must conduct interviews, carry out research and then present the completed copy to the Subeditor. Some Reporters will specialise, for example in politics or business news. Those Reporters working in broadcasting may have contracts for both television and radio. It is also possible that Reporters may present and record their own news item.

- Interviewing skills
- Ability to operate recording equipment

Press Photographers
Photographers may be generalist or specialist (eg fashion) and hold staff positions or be freelance. They provide the pictures to illustrate

the news items. They may also supply captions and stories to their photos.
- Photographic skills and experience

Features Writer
A feature is an article that is not news. Writers are often specialist, eg in the arts , travel or medicine, and they are nearly always freelance.
- Specialist knowledge
- Writing skills

Special Correspondents
Special Correspondents are diplomatic, foreign and political Reporters, who go to trouble spots as news is breaking or who are stationed in prominent cities such as Washington and Moscow to provide 'on-the-spot' stories.
- Specialist knowledge
- Sensitivity and experience

Newsreader
The Newsreader helps put together the news reports that he or she will read on air. Timing is crucial and so is the necessity to deliver accurate bulletins.
- Current affairs knowledge
- Calm, clear voice and good pronunciation
- Professional attitude
- Editorial skills

Page Designer
The Page Designer prepares the text layout on computer by using a DTP system. The work will include designing the text to house-style and placing illustrations.
- DTP training and experience
- Good visual sense
- Portfolio of work

Related journalism occupations
- Press support organisations
- Government press departments
- Picture agencies and libraries
- Press and public relations (see above)
- Advertising copywriting
- Book publicity

- Book publishing (see below)
- Critic
- Writer
- Information officer

☐ BOOK PUBLISHING

Many individual publishing companies have merged or been taken over by larger houses which are made up of several smaller firms known as 'imprints'. Nevertheless, new smaller publishing companies, which mainly specialise (eg in education or children's picture books) are often being set up. Job roles in publishing do overlap – especially in smaller companies. Job titles for a particular job function will often vary from company to company. The larger publishers are more likely to have distinct departments covering Editorial, Art/Design, Production, Sales, Marketing and Publicity while smaller companies will tend to use freelancers for the more specialist functions. For this reason the information given below is presented under departmental headings and job functions.

The work areas you may consider if you wish to pursue a career in publishing are:
- General publishers
- Specialist publishers
- Small presses
- Packagers
- Multimedia (see page 29)
- Picture agencies and libraries
- Editorial and research services

Editorial Department

Editorial is the most popular career choice for those wishing to enter the publishing industry, but has the least job opportunities. It is this department which transforms the author's manuscript – using freelancers where necessary – into publishable form. There are opportunities for Editorial Assistants/Secretaries in this department to assist in the editorial process in larger publishing houses or where budget allows.
- General knowledge
- Good memory
- Organisational skills

Commissioning Editor

The Commissioning Editor has to find and buy new work, by looking for authors and assessing the manuscripts sent in. He or she will negotiate the clauses in the contract with the author, prepare information about the book for booksellers and libraries, and brief other departments for editing and production.

- Tact
- Ability to spot good potential
- Editorial skills

Desk Editor

The Desk Editor prepares manuscripts for the typesetter – copyediting, ie ensuring the book is well-structured, accurate in its content, has continuity, fits house-style and is grammatically correct. The in-house Desk Editor may commission freelance copyeditors and proofreaders, and will liaise with authors.

- Knowledge of editing and proof correction symbols
- Attention to detail
- Good grasp of English and writing skills

Literary Agent

The Literary Agent takes on authors and gets them the best possible deal with the most suitable publisher. They may also get the author's work into television, radio and merchandise. They offer business management and advice, they may be self-employed and could specialise in a particular area.

- Knowledge of media law
- Financial awareness
- Editorial skills
- Negotiation skills
- Excellent experience of industry

Art/Design Department

The job of the art/design department is to create an image of a book that will enable it to be targeted at the people most likely to buy it, from the cover illustration to typeface and layout, from chapter headings to the use of internal photographs, illustrations and diagrams. Companies that produce highly illustrated books may have a more structured art/design department. This department may also commission freelance illustrators and photographers and will be responsible for the in-house style and the company's visual identity.

- Creativity

● Art/design training

Illustrator/Photographer
Freelance Illustrators and Photographers will be commissioned to
contribute work to a particular publication by the Art Director or
picture researcher.
● Art/photographic training
● Ability to translate text into pictures
● Portfolio of work

Picture Researcher
This job entails finding suitable pictures to illustrate books/covers
from photographic libraries, government departments, press
agencies, museums and galleries. The Picture Researcher is also
responsible for going through the legal procedures necessary in order
to publish the picture, which includes negotiating fees and returning
the picture after use. The Picture Researcher must work within a
budget.
● Specialist knowledge and training
● Attention to detail
● Financial skills
● Relevant experience

Book Designer/Typesetter
The Typesetter is responsible for the overall look of the book. The
Typesetter takes the edited text on disk and uses a DTP programme
to design and print out a layout to be used by the printer. This
involves choosing fonts, designing headings etc and integrating
pictures with text. The Typesetter must ensure that the typographic
specifications are such that the book is the right number of pages.
● Creativity
● Attention to detail
● Training in graphics or printing industry experience

Production Department

The function of the production department is to manufacture the
highest possible quality books, given a set budget and within the
deadline specified. A budget is allocated to each book by working out
how much it is going to cost to produce. This involves deciding on
paper weight and quality, size of publication and number of
illustrations. Deals must also be negotiated with the paper
producers, typesetters and printers. Some companies may employ

someone solely as a paper and print buyer, however this function is often the responsibility of the Production Manager who must know technical details such as how each grade of paper will affect the printing. Some publishing companies use the same paper suppliers and printers each time, others negotiate with different companies for each commission. There is considerable overlap with the design department and in some companies production and design come under one department.

- Good negotiation skills
- Knowledge of printing methods
- Ability to prioritise

Production Controller/Assistant
The Production Controller works from the edited typescript stage through to the end product. Work involves organising typesetting, proofreading and printing. The Production Controller also checks the 'running sheets' (the printed pages before they are bound into a book) to ensure quality of the final product.

- Diplomacy
- Attention to detail
- Ability to work to deadlines

Sales, Marketing and Publicity Department

Sales, marketing and publicity work closely to bring the attention of potential buyers to the books and their rights. This means circulating information about the book via posters, shop window displays, and catalogues, in addition to initiating reviews of the book in the media, organising author signings – and any other method of boosting sales. Some companies, particularly directory and business publishers, will also have an advertising sales function, for selling advertising space in the company's books to any appropriate organisations.

- Excellent business sense
- Ability to motivate and excite others

Sales and Marketing Director
The Sales and Marketing Director deals with the budgets and strategies for marketing the books and decides on the cover price in addition to managing the large accounts such as Waterstones or WH Smiths. He or she will also give presentations to explain and preview new titles. The **Key Accounts Manager** is responsible for the smaller accounts and will also work out new ways of generating

sales. The Sales and Marketing Director is also responsible for the Sales Reps (see below).
- Managerial and financial skills
- Bookselling experience

Sales Representatives
Sales Reps visit bookshops in their specified region on a regular basis to sell the booklist. The Reps are given information on the new books and authors and they sell to bookshops, libraries etc using information sheets and the company catalogue. An Educational Rep is someone who visits educational establishments and sells books.
- Knowledge and enthusiasm for books
- Willingness to travel
- Experience in bookshop or selling

Publicity and Marketing
Personnel in this area will write the 'blurbs' for the book jackets, think up marketing proposals and campaigns, buy advertising space and get editorial coverage in the media – writing advertising copy and press releases. They will also arrange book signings, organise shop, exhibition and fair promotions, commission design for advertisements and work out promotion budgets for books. It is necessary to get the bookshops and libraries to take on the books and encourage the public to buy them. Work in this area involves both promotions and public relations and personnel may specialise in one or the other.

Further job functions

Secretary/Assistant
The Secretary/Assistant job is an entry level grade. The work involves typing and administration and ensuring deadlines are met. The Secretary may also read manuscripts as part of the preselection process and proofread the jacket/cover and manuscripts. It is also the job of the secretary to answer queries and liaise with the other departments.
- Diplomacy
- Secretarial/administration skills

Royalties Manager
The Royalties Manager will pay the authors, illustrators and other publishers the money owed to them from the sale of their work. The Royalties Manager must work out the money owed from the number

of sales and make payments, usually twice yearly. They must be able to deal with the inevitable queries that arise.
- Ability to work under pressure
- Knowledgeable about VAT and tax agreements
- Accountancy training

Contracts and Rights Manager/Copyright and Permissions Editor

The selling of the subsidiary rights of a book according to the publishing contract is the responsibility of the Rights Manager. This includes translation, merchandising and coedition rights. The Contracts Manager is responsible for drawing up contracts between the Authors and Publishers and other legal aspects of book publishing including permitting passages of text or illustrations to be used by other publishers from its copyright works.
- Financial and legal knowledge
- Negotiation skills
- Experience

Related book publishing occupations
- Bookseller
- Newspapers and periodicals (see Journalism)
- Library services
- Literary support organisations
- Translators
- Promotions and public relations
- Indexers
- Lexicography

☐ MULTIMEDIA

Skillset (the industry training organisation for broadcast, film and video) defines 'multimedia' as:

> *'A fusion of computing and audio-visual technologies to combine any or all of the following media: Text, Audio, Graphics, Still Pictures, Animation and Moving Pictures.'*

The employers in this field are:

- Book and magazine publishers
- Design and presentation houses
- Multimedia production companies

- UK and international corporations
- Financial services

The following job functions are typical of those found in a real-life multimedia studio.

Producer
The Producer is in charge of the multimedia project. He or she talks to the client to discuss what is required and negotiate the financial deal, oversee the design of the project and ensure it is both thoroughly tested and delivered on time.
- Managerial skills
- Good negotiation
- Relevant experience

Graphic Artist
Creates all the graphical material used for a project. He or she will use software packages on Apple Macintosh or PC such as *Adobe Photoshop* to generate the necessary graphics. The Graphic Artist will have a large influence on the 'look and feel' of the product.
- CAD (Computer Aided Design) skills
- Expertise in relevant software
- Training in art/design

Video Engineer
Responsible for editing and digitising video from various tape sources, the Video Engineer will use equipment such as a *Media 100* system.
- Technical skills
- Video training
- Relevant experience

Sound Engineer
The sound samples for a multimedia title are sourced by the Sound Engineer, who will edit and digitise them for playback on the PC.
- Ability to link information to sound
- Sound recording skills
- Technical training

Software Engineer
The Software Engineer creates the multimedia application using programming applications such as C/C++ and also authoring tools such as Macromedia's *Director*. The role requires the integration of

text, graphics, video and sound provided by the rest of the team.
- Ability to link the necessary components
- Relevant software expertise and experience
- Technical training

Tester
The Tester is the person responsible for quality assurance. He or she checks the content of a title, its functionality and that it works on all the hardware platforms required.
- Excellent computer skills
- Relevant training
- Knowledge and experience of the industry

CASE STUDY

Joy Peraud, Trainee Reporter for the Greenford and Northolt Gazette

Joy Peraud is a Trainee Reporter for the *Greenford and Northolt Gazette*. Prior to her recruitment for this job, she worked as an Editorial Assistant on the *Hammersmith, Fulham and Shepherd's Bush Gazette*.

Joy originally did a degree in Psychology, which she 'fell into' because she was good at sciences at school, and it was not until she left university that she became determined to follow a career in journalism. By then she had used up her grant quota, so could not go on to do a journalism course: 'It really boiled down to a question of money, and I couldn't see a way into journalism, so I took a job working in the classified section of the Advertising Department at the newspaper company where I work now. After a while, selling advertising space became really boring. I couldn't stand it anymore, so I handed in my notice.'

This turned out to be a good move for Joy. The Editor of the *Hammersmith,*

Fulham and Shepherd's Bush Gazette had seen Joy around, although they had never spoke to one another. Joy knew he was looking for an Editorial Assistant, and on her last day in the advertising job, they got talking. She explained that she was leaving and he told her that he would be needing someone for two half-days a week and asked if she would be interested. 'I got the job because he had seen me around the building and it helped that I already knew a bit about the company. The job wouldn't have been advertised externally.'

Her job as Editorial Assistant at the *Hammersmith Fulham and Shepherd's Bush Gazette* newsdesk entailed doing about four different jobs at the same time – these were mainly clerical, typing copy etc. It was while doing this job that she began to write 'bits and pieces' for the paper. 'A vacancy then came up on the *Greenford and Northolt Gazette* newsdesk and my Editor asked me if I would be interested. I started last December. It

31

wasn't actually a trainee post as such, that didn't happen until three months after I started, and everything I've learnt, I learnt on the job and of course with the help of my colleagues.'

Joy was never asked about her degree in any of the jobs she applied for. But she doesn't think it was totally irrelevant. 'Psychology is, after all, about people, and working with different people all the time,

interviewing them and so on, means that my degree has been put to good use.'

Joy admits her work came about by contacts and word of mouth once she had got into publications via advertising sales. It took her just over two years to achieve her goal, and since the first edition of *Getting into the Media*, she has become Staff Writer for the trade magazine *Medeconomics*.

THE SALARIES

☐ WHAT YOU CAN EXPECT TO EARN

The following salary details are a guide only to the sort of wages you could expect to be paid for working in the media. The salaries will vary considerably, and unfortunately not always in your favour.

Television, film and radio

The rates below are those recommended by BECTU (Broadcasting, Entertainment and Cinematograph Theatres Union). The different jobs are divided into 13 different grades and a job title example from each group has been given.

Grade	Job Title	Per 40 Hours a Week
01	Runner	£220.00
02	SFX (special effects) Trainee	£286.00
03	Secretary	£330.00
04	Assistant Accountant	£363.00
05	Rigger/Camera Cabler	£423.50
06	Make-up/Hair Assistant	£456.50
07	Wardrobe Assistant	£495.00
08	Sound Engineer	£610.50
09	Floor Manager	£660.00
10	Senior Researcher	£687.50
11	Art Director	£770.00
12	Cameraperson, Lighting	£907.50
13	Director	£1056.00

Work is generally freelance and you will not necessarily be employed for 12 months of the year. You should take this into account when assessing your likely annual income.

Journalism and publishing

The following minimum rates are those recommended by the NUJ (the National Union of Journalists) for freelance workers. The NUJ says it is up to Journalists to negotiate the best deal they can with their employees. Rates vary according to whether you are working for a national or local paper or magazine. Don't forget that these are recommended rates so it does not mean you will always get them, particularly in book publishing where NUJ rates are largely ignored. There is a huge variation in the amounts publishing houses pay (or very specialist editors demand).

Writers
Rates vary according to the medium worked in. Authors should expect royalties in the region of 7.5% to 10% of the cover price of the book. Magazines are classed into groups from A (eg *Marie Claire*) to D (eg *Nursing Times*). Journalists working on a Group A magazine should be paid at least £350 per 1000 words and £130 per 1000 words for a Group D magazine. The rate for a national newspaper is £200 minimum per 1000 words for a news story and £500 for an exclusive regardless of word length. Provincial (local weekly) papers will pay £1.70 for up to ten lines and 17 pence per line thereafter.

Subbing, production and book editing
Rates for books are: Proofreading £12.95 per hour; Subediting and Rewriting £15.40 per hour; Reading fees £13 per hour. (Although these are NUJ minimum rates, they really are the maximum a freelancer can expect to earn in book publishing.) Daily rates for subbing on magazines are £90–£200 and for a seven hour shift on a national newspaper £110–140 and £230 for a 13 hour shift on a regional or provincial paper.

Press and public relations
For a non-commercial organisation £150 per day for press office work and £146 per day for electronic page production. Writers can expect to earn in the region of £150–£250 per 1000 words.

Broadcasting
The rate for Reporters working in regional television and radio is £105 per day and £83 per day for local radio. These rates are in accordance with the BBC Freelance Guidelines. Interviews and talks by professional broadcasters (interviewer or interviewee) for up to five minutes will earn £48 and £29 for non-professionals.

Photography
In a UK or one language book a photographer can expect to receive £72 for a quarter of a page and £372 for a wrap round. In Group A

magazine, the rates for a photograph on the cover is £480 compared with £200 for a black and white photo on a Group C and D magazine cover. In national newspapers the rate is £65 for 1/32 of a page and £60 for a mug shot for press and PR. The rate for a single transmission of between four and ten seconds in broadcasting is £100. Daily rates for photographers vary considerably from £50 per day for a provincial paper to £675 a day for studio work.

Design
For books the NUJ rate for designing a jacket or cover is a minimum of £309 (although about two-thirds of this rate is more realistic) plus expenses and £95 to £120 per day for magazines.

Digital/electronic media
For non-exclusive re-use of material on a Website, freelancers should charge 50% of original fee or 50% of gross income from consumers if applicable. For CD-ROMS freelancers should charge approximately 50% of original fee. When the material is original, rates for setting up pages on existing Websites and editing on Websites are a minimum of £40 per hour (and the same for editing CD-ROMS) for commercial companies and £50 and hour for managing Website production.

Picture editing and research
Basic picture research for books is £15 to £17 an hour, £105 per day for Group C and D magazines and £110 a shift or day for national newspapers. For broadcasting the rate is £17 per hour and for press and PR for commercial companies £25 per hour.

Illustration and cartoons
For books, magazines and newspapers the rates are in accordance with that of photographic work. An illustrator should expect to be paid a minimum of £262 for a book jacket or £130 a day. For press and PR the rate for an illustration for a commercial organisation is £125 for a quarter of a page. Cartoons for Group A magazines in black and white are £94 and £60 for a Group D, and black and white cartoons of one column in a national paper £100.

The typical starting salary for a job in the media (except publishing) is £13,600 per annum, even if you are a graduate. This is below the average starting salary of £14,400. In publishing starting salaries are in the region of £11,000–£13,000.

EDUCATION AND TRAINING

☐ BEYOND 16

Getting media qualifications through further education – A-levels, BTEC, City and Guilds, Foundation courses, and perhaps GCSEs and Access courses – can provide you with that vital stepping stone to gaining entry on to a degree course. At this level, courses also generally offer a high level of practical involvement, which is essential to developing your skills in your chosen area and gaining a taste of what a job in the media might really entail.

For a comprehensive list of further education courses in film, broadcasting, journalism, animation and graphic design, see the British Film Institute's annual directory, *Media Courses UK.*

☐ TO DO A DEGREE OR NOT?

Although it has been said that employers tend to be more concerned with a person's experience than his or her qualifications, most would agree that a degree can help you in more ways than one. It won't necessarily aid you in getting your first job (although nowadays graduates with experience are more likely to be selected than non-graduates with experience, even for the most menial of jobs) but it can help you later on in your career as far as promotion and moving on are concerned. It also gives you the ability to be more critical about what you see, hear and do, so that you are able to bring a more constructive approach to your work, or branch out on your own.

Time to mature

Spending three or four years at university also gives you time to mature as a person and so be better equipped to enter the job market. In many cases employers will be looking for someone who is slightly maturer than school-leaving age (the BBC never takes on people straight from school). If you are of school-leaving age, it might be possible to gain some valuable work experience before embarking on a degree course. Working on a voluntary basis at, for example, a local radio station may also be valuable in gaining information about universities and degrees that are recognised by the industry, and may save you from making a mistake in your choice.

Selection criteria

Nowadays there are numerous media and communications degrees on offer, but if you are interested in pursuing a practical career in film, television or radio, it is essential that you are selective about choosing which university to go to. There are also growing numbers of publishing degree courses, and while most entrants (except those in specialist areas, eg graphic design) do not hold such qualifications, these courses are worth considering. There are several criteria that you should consider when making your choice:

● *The practical component*
How much of the degree is composed of practical, 'hands-on' training?

● *Work placements*
Does the course offer organised work placements within the media industry or will you have to look for work experience independently?

● *Professional staff*
Have the teaching staff worked in the industry themselves? Do they continue to do so? Are they in touch with what is happening in the industry today and are they familiar with new technologies? Do the staff keep up-to-date with their knowledge/training?

● *Equipment*
How modern is the equipment that is used at the university? Technology is changing rapidly and equipment is expensive, so you cannot expect an educational institution to be kitted out with all the latest gadgets, but it does need to be reasonably modern for you to benefit from training on it. In addition, will you have access to information about the most up-to-date technology?

● *Validation*
What validation or accreditation does the course have? What have previous students gone on to do? Have they managed to break into the industry?

- *NVQs*
  Will the course be based on NVQ standards?

NB If you have ambitions to become an engineer in the media, it is worth checking out which colleges can offer you broadcasting options or excellent studio facilities.

Undergraduate courses

Due to recent changes in higher education, universities must now put more emphasis on the marketplace and offer prospective students courses which are popular, in order to gain funding. This has resulted in many more media courses being on offer, but the level of practical work varies considerably from course to course.

Entry to a degree course usually require five GCSEs – Grade C or above – and two A-levels. Entry requirements are different for mature students, when formal qualifications may not be necessary.

What about a non-media related degree?

It is not always necessary to take a 'media' degree in order to follow a career in this industry. The way the industry has changed in recent years means that companies desperately need people who know about, for example, how the Inland Revenue functions, VAT, how to secure loans, raise money, and so on. In other words, financial qualifications will help you find a job in the media too. Maybe you can get onto a degree programme that combines accountancy with practical media production. Alternative routes of study you might like to consider are: Media Law, Information Technology, Drama, Art and Design.

Lucy Wade, Broadcast Assistant at BBC Radio 5 Live

Lucy Wade graduated from Thames Valley University with a BA in Design and Media Management (DAMM). Prior to her appointment at Radio 5 Live she worked for 18 months as a Researcher/ Production Assistant for BBC Radio 4's foreign news programme, *From Our Own Correspondent.*

Lucy knew from the age of 15 she wanted to work in radio, so she obtained as much work experience as possible at her local hospital radio, and *BBC Radio York.* Here she worked for free, doing anything she could – sweeping the floor, making the tea and answering the phone. In 1989 she got accepted on to the DAMM degree course. The fact that she had already won a broadcasting competition helped in gaining her a place. She chose to do the DAMM degree because of her interest in radio and the fact that the degree included a practical media component.

When Lucy first applied for the position at Radio 4 on *From Our Own Correspondent,* she was able to arrange a preliminary meeting with the person who was to be her boss. 'I was lucky that I got this first job at Radio 4. I came down to meet the person who was going to be my boss before the interview. If you can, you must go and meet the people who could be your employers. It impresses them if you get on. When I met him, we got on brilliantly well. He basically gave me loads of tips about the interview and it got me the job.'

Applying for her second job at the BBC wasn't so easy. Lucy had to compete against thousands of other applicants. Filling out an application form was only the first stage. This was followed by an interview, then completion of a research topic, and then a second round of interviews. 'They gave you such a hard time at your interview about your research topic. They totally picked mine to pieces and I thought, "No way have I got this job," but I didn't think I'd done a bad research job; they were just seeing how I reacted, I think.'

Lucy did get the job. She thinks that one of the reasons she was successful was because she came across confidently in the interview. Her job is permanent and at first her working hours were 8.30am to 6.30pm every day, without a lunch break.

Any advice?
Get as much work experience as possible: 'It's absolutely vital. I wouldn't have got in without it. Go to your local radio station, go to hospital radio, pester them like mad, sit on the doorstep if necessary. Once you've got that experience, do a media course if possible and even a postgraduate course – the news trainee schemes are excellent – and keep knocking on the BBC's door!'

Since the first edition of *Getting into the Media,* Lucy has gone on to work as a Broadcast Assistant for Radio 5 Live's *Inside Edge* programme.

Shay Leonard freelances for an art department of a film production company

When Shay decided he wanted to work in film he knew he had two choices – to work his way in or go to school first. He opted to do a BA in Film Studies and French at the University of North London and graduated in 1996. For Shay the degree was too theoretical and not enough hands-on. However, it gave him time to make sure he was committed to working in film, and the advantage of developing a second language in case the opportunity arose of working on a European coproduction.

He works in an art department on films, employed by the Production Designer to paint and design sets and make and work with props.

Shay has worked on several feature films, all of which he got through contacts. His first, *Pervirella* was a low-budget film – in other words, nobody was paid. It was good work experience though and through this he got further work on other films. This led to meeting more people who had contacts working in the film industry. 'People talk about having a lucky break – but you have to realise that when you are getting work experience on a low-budget film, so are 25–50 other people, and so the ones who have been working longer are the ones who are more likely to get work.'

Shay's first paid work was on *Lockstock* and *Two Smoking Barrels* when he got what are known as half wages, when you are paid half your normal wages weekly and the other half on completion of the film. This is different to deferred payment which is when you are only paid if the film makes money. Shay worked a 72 hour week, six days a week, 12 hours a day. 'I worked from 8am until 8pm which is pretty standard for the film industry. We didn't really do much overtime, which was good, because I wouldn't have been paid for it. I was getting a decent wage of £300 a week on half pay, so £600 a week in total which isn't bad. Just a bit less the the union rate I think.'

Shay has also recently worked as a runner on the Pulp video *This is Hard Core*. 'The advantage of being a runner on set is you have a lot of time when you are not really doing very much so you can choose to help out in an area that interests you. I helped out in the Art Department, but if you were interested in becoming a camera operator you could assist in this area, and those people will keep asking you back to help them so you will learn more. It can work to your advantage if you want to learn about film making.'

He also has some useful information to bear in mind for runners. 'I've only just recently learned how to drive and most of the time you must have a car to be taken on as a runner, but if there is a choice of two runners on set and only one of you drives you may find that all you spend doing for eight weeks is just driving around picking up things and therefore you don't really get to see or learn much. You're just a taxi service. So while in some ways it's better not to have a car, you probably won't be employed unless you've got one!'

Was his degree useful in getting work? 'No one has ever asked about my degree, so although it might look good on a CV, it hasn't proved very helpful. All my work has been through contacts – just after I graduated I sent off 50 CVs and blindly called up production companies. I got 15 responses saying they'd keep my details on file.'

Shay has two possible films lined up for later this year, one working for standby props for the next Peter Greenaway film, and the other working for the Production Designer on a film starring Martin Clunes, so he is happy with the way his career is progressing.

Any advice?
'You have to be totally committed to working in film. I've read a lot about these extrovert personalities who want to work in film who get in by constant hassling. I'm just not like that. I would never have had the confidence to sit on someone's doorstep to get a job. I've worked my way in by proving myself and getting along with people and getting work by getting experience. You just need to work on short films and low-budget films and get experience. Find out what's going to be in production and get in contact with the relevant production companies and see if they need some help.'

LIFE AFTER UNIVERSITY

You may feel that at the end of your degree course you need some additional training, and there are various options open to you. Please note, you do not always require a degree in order to be accepted on the courses or training schemes outlined below:

- Postgraduate courses
- FT2
- In-house training scheme, eg. BBC and ITV
- Short courses such as Future In Films
- National Vocational Qualifications

☐ POSTGRADUATE COURSES

The nature of postgraduate courses is extremely varied; some have Fine Art emphasis, while others are industry oriented. Applicants are normally expected to have completed an undergraduate course. For a comprehensive list of postgraduate courses in broadcasting, film, journalism, animation and graphic design see the BFI's Directory *Media Courses UK*.

There are also several postgraduate journalism courses. These usually run for only a few weeks, and can be quite expensive. They are often listed in Monday's *Media Guardian* and other relevant journals. The Journalism Training Centre in Mitcham offers a 15-week journalism course in which students will train for their NVQ Core Skills Certificates.

In addition, the National Council for the Training of Journalists (NCTJ) runs three distance learning courses which lead to NVQs in Newspaper or Periodical Journalism. Contact the NCTJ for further information.

Journalism skills are also taught in nine weeks by PMA Training. The course leads to the NVQ and costs in the region of £2000. You should qualify for a 23% vocational tax relief. At the end of the course, PMA also helps you get a job, and as more than half of journalism jobs are never advertised, the contacts PMA can supply are very useful.

Media Production Facilities offers courses in TV journalism (as well as technical courses in light, sound, camera operations and computer graphics) and the University of Westminster does a postgraduate diploma in journalism – Broadcast and Periodical – for people from ethnic minorities. The NUJ has also set up the George Viner Memorial Fund for people from ethnic minorities who wish to pursue a full-time course in journalism but lack the finances to do so.

The only place in the country offering a specialised course in photojournalism and press photography which is recognised by the paper industry is Sheffield College. The cost of the 36-week course, with six weeks work experience, is approximately £1000, and the college claims to have a 100% placement.

A two-day picture researcher course (and any other training relevant to the publishing industry) is held at the Publishing Training Centre in Wandsworth and the London College of Printing offers a one-day course.

There are also a number of postgraduate courses in publishing available at higher education institutions across the country. Consult the prospectuses in the reference section of your local library.

☐ FILM AND TELEVISION FREELANCE TRAINING

Another option to follow is the FT2 route. You do not necessarily need to have completed a graduate programme first, but you must be over 18 in order to qualify. In addition, you must be able to demonstrate a commitment to the film and television industry and all that entails, and, as you have probably guessed, the competition is fierce.

Film and Television Freelance Training, or FT2 as it is more commonly known, provides new entrant training in the junior construction, technical and production grades for the film and television industry. It provides training and NVQs, which are funded

and managed by the industry, in: New Entrant Technical Training
Programme, Setcrafts Apprenticeship Training Scheme, Independent
Companies Research Training Scheme, Freelance NVQ Assessment
Service. Representatives from AFVPA, BBC, BECTU, Channel 4,
ITVA and PACT are on FT2's Council of Management (see Directory
for full names of organisations).

☐ IN-HOUSE TRAINEE SCHEMES

Trainee schemes are courses or apprenticeships offered in-house by
the industry employers, which all operate equal opportunities
policies. There is not always a guarantee, however, that you will
eventually get a job with the same company you train with.
Examples of companies that offer traineeships are the BBC and
Reuters news agency.

The trainee schemes are a good way of entering the industry, in that
you are trained on the job for a certain period of time – although
with the introduction of the NVQs, the training period will last as
long as it takes for you to prove your competence at the job. What is
more, you get paid while being trained. This is generally a modest
fee, but may be reasonably good for first-time jobbers.

Adverts for the training schemes are generally advertised in
Monday's *Media Guardian* and other relevant journals, so keep your
eyes peeled but, as usual, expect the competition to be extremely
tough. In 1998 the Regional Broadcast Trainee Scheme offered by
the BBC attracted 16,500 requests for application forms of which
around 25% are expected to reply – that is over 4000. (The
application form is designed to encourage only those people with a
realistic chance to apply.) There are usually only between eight and
fourteen candidates selected. Bearing this in mind, you will realise
the necessity of having relevant work experience and the ability to
demonstrate a commitment to and interest in the industry.

Another example of a training scheme is Fourfit – a two-year
production scheme for people from ethnic groups run by Channel 4.
The next uptake is for summer 1999.

In some cases, training will be given if you become employed by a
company. At IPC Magazines, for example, journalists who come to
work on a magazine with less than two years' experience are

classified as Trainee Journalists. From their first day of employment they will be given in-house training which lasts for around two years. The method of competence-based training they use at IPC Magazines is very similar to the Journalism NVQs. It is not a requirement to have a degree to become a trainee, but a passion for journalism must be demonstrated.

☐ SHORT SPECIALISED COURSES

The description of the Panico Media Workshop courses are used as an example of another type of avenue available to you. It exemplifies the fee-paying short course route. Some short courses are subsidised by local authorities, Regional Arts Boards and European funding, while others are run commercially. In some cases there are conditions of entry on to short courses; for example, that you are already employed in the industry. In the case of Panico Media Workshop, there is no selection procedure, although you may be invited in to meet the director to see if the course is appropriate to your needs. The Foundation course costs £580.

The Foundation, Certificate and Advanced courses run by Panico Media Workshop are designed to give practical hands-on experience under the guidance of top professional filmmakers who are still active in the industry today. Indeed, among the post-production credits at Panico Studios are *A Fish Called Wanda*, and *The Fisher King*, and because the studios are owned by various members of the Monty Python team, students get to use footage, such as *Life of Brian*, for analysing filmmaking.

On completion of the Foundation course, students are expected to have acquired enough knowledge and skills to be able to undertake their own productions in the workshop in addition to questioning whether they are suited to the tough competitive life of the film industry. Open to people of all ages and abilities, the Foundation course is largely practical and takes place over five days.

Projects may range from 35mm or 16mm shorts for entry into film festivals, video productions for community use, pieces of work to be used as pilots to support applications for funding jobs, or entry to higher courses such as those run by the National School of Film and Television.

Panico Media Workshop also runs an advanced course, and all the workshop and formal course activities are supervised and used for assessment. Additionally, it helps ex-students organise and shoot their own projects by supplying equipment, processing and technical back-up. For further information, contact Panico Media Workshop (see Directory).

☐ OTHER SHORT COURSES

For more information on other short courses, obtain the latest edition of *A Listing of Short Courses in Film, Media and Multimedia* published by the BFI. Also see the list of workshops in the Listings section at the end of this brochure, many of which offer training. Some short courses are specifically geared to meet the needs of those people who are currently under-represented in the industry.

Connections Communication Centre in Hammersmith is fully wheelchair accessible and offer courses in video production from single camera operation to sound recording and technology. Cultural Partnerships runs courses in video and radio production course to students under 24 who are unemployed. It is the priority of Cultural Partnerships to encourage women and young people from the Black and Asian communities to apply.

The Publishing Training Centre (previously Book House) provides over 100 short training courses each year on all aspects of book publishing at every level. These include editorial, production, marketing, rights, computer skills, finance and many more. *Chapterhouse Publishing* offers a number of correspondence courses, particularly in editorial skills (see Directory for address).

☐ S/NVQs

'We're going to need some kind of recognised standard as the market becomes more fragmented and more freelance.'
Phil Redmond, *Brookside* creator

NVQs (National Vocational Qualifications) and SVQs (Scottish Vocational Qualifications) are about actually proving you can do the job, rather than simply writing or talking about it. There are five different levels of S/NVQ, from basic (Level 1) to professional (Level 5). S/NVQ assessment takes place in the workplace or a simulated working environment. Awards are made if someone can perform the tasks and meet the standards of competence required, regardless of how that person has trained.

People can train for S/NVQs at their own pace, and any abilities they may already have are recognised without the need for retraining. Lead bodies produce and set the standards for S/NVQs. The S/NVQs for periodical and newspaper journalism are already in place. The Newspaper Society is the lead body for the journalism S/NVQs. The broadcast, film and video S/NVQs are currently being developed and implemented and the lead body for these is Skillset.

There are no longer any S/NVQs for publishing. The industry decided they were too bureaucratic, and did not like the idea of a national qualification. However, the standards set by S/NVQs is appreciated, and they continue to be used as a guide for job descriptions, appraisals and so on. The possibility of an alternative qualification is being looked into, as is the potential for an institute of publishing. Should you require further information contact the Publishing Training Centre (see Directory).

Since their launch in 1995 there have been, at the time of going to press, 600 candidates for either units or full qualifications in the broadcast, film and video sector. Targets are being set to keep the implementation of these S/NVQs moving forward, but it will be some years before the true impact of S/NVQs on the industry is felt, including the effect they will have on gender balance, disability and so on.

S/NVQs will not solve the 'little black book syndrome' overnight, nor will they ensure a job, but they do provide an industry standard for employers to use when assessing potential employees. As S/NVQs begin to be recognised by the industry they will become an important factor in identifying competence in freelancers.

Skillset S/NVQs

The table on the next page lists the accredited S/NVQs in the broadcast, film and video area at the time of going to press:

S/NVQ		Level
Camera/	Camera Assistance	2
Lighting	Camera Operation and Assistance	3
	Camera Direction	4
	Lighting Operation	3
	Lighting Provision and Coordination (Electrical)	4
	Lighting Direction	4
Sound	Sound Assistance*	2
	Sound Operation*	3
	Sound Direction*	4
Production/	Production	3
Journalism	Production*	4
	Production Research*	3
	Broadcast Journalism*	4
Makeup/	Art Direction	4
Costume/	Make-up/Hair	3
Design	Make-up/Hair Design and Realisation	4
	Costume Supervision and Maintenance	3
	Costume Design and Realisation	4
Post-	Electronic Post-Production Support	2
Production/	Film Post-Production Support	2
Animation	Editing	3
	Editing	4
	Animation Assistance	3
	Animation Realisation	4
Studio	Video Tape Operations	2
Operations	Vision Control	3
	Vision Mixing	3

* Also applicable to radio

The following S/NVQs are the most recent ones to be accredited:

S/NVQ	Level
Film Projection	2
Graphic Design for Moving Images	3
Graphic Design for Moving Images	4
Motion Picture Film Processing	3
Properties	2
Properties	3
Properties	4
Set Dressing	2
Radio Production	3
Radio Production	4
Painting and Decorating (Construction)	3
Wood Occupations (Construction)	4
Plastering Solid and Fibrous (Construction)	3

For further information on media S/NVQs, contact Kate O'Connor, the NVQ Director of Standards and Qualifications at Skillset.

Journalism S/NVQs

NVQs in Newspaper Journalism are awarded by the RSA Examinations Board in partnership with the Newspaper Qualifications Council. SVQs are awarded by the Scottish Qualifications Authority (SQA). These are as follows:

S/NVQ	Level
Newspaper Journalism (Writing)	4
Newspaper Journalism (Production Journalism)	4
Newspaper Journalism (Press Photography)	4
Newspaper Journalism (Graphics Journalism)	3

Periodical NVQs

NVQs for periodicals are also awarded by the RSA. There is no Scottish equivalent. These are:

NVQ	Level
Periodical and Journalism (Writing and Subbing)	4
Periodical and Journalism (Advertising Production)	2
Periodical and Journalism (Advertising Production)	3
Periodical and Journalism (Advertising Production)	4

In the meantime, if you are looking for a course to gain further skills, consider those that will lead to NVQ assessment. These qualifications may prove very useful in the future.

CASE STUDY

Celine Nava, Finance and Sales Administrator at Barefoot Books Ltd

Celine Nava studied ancient, medieval and modern history at degree level in England before starting her quest to work in the book publishing industry. She returned to her native France and sent her CV to a local publishers, Actes Sud, offering to work for them for free. She was accepted and worked there for eight months where she read about 20 manuscripts a day as part of the preselection process. Her job, to decide whether the manuscripts should be further read or discarded, was paid for in books.

After eight months at Actes Sud she was offered a job, but decided to return to England. Someone from Actes Sud knew the head of the literary department at the French Embassy and this is where she began four more months of work experience. This time her work included the more financial aspects of publishing.

In 1997 she went to the London Book Fair where she met a printer's agent. One of the agent's customers was Barefoot Books and it was through the agent that Celine landed her first job as Finance and Sales Administrator. 'It was sheer luck that I got the job. The London Book Fair is a good place to go if you want to work in the publishing industry.' Celine was given an interview on the strength of personal recommendation, before the job had even been advertised. 'My experience in editorial and production was very useful, and I got on well with the interviewer. I was taken on for a four-month trial period.' Celine's job entails making royalty payments to authors as well as to chase money from copublishers. She also monitors sales and checks financial reports with the distributor.

Celine is currently training as assistant to the managing director and will be instrumental in opening an office in the USA. She is focusing on eventually working in distribution and production in a managerial capacity.

So what does Celine see as the vital attributes for working in the publishing industry? 'You have to try really hard as hundreds of people want to work in publishing, and you mustn't have high expectations. Expect to start off on a low salary. A graduate can expect to earn around £12,000.' Celine pinpoints work experience as being extremely useful, not just for the experience but as a way of meeting people who can help you get work, 'Network your way in and you will get the relevant referees. You also need to be really open-minded and willing to work long hours'. Celine usually works a 10-hour day. 'A good amount of general cultural, artistic knowledge is a necessity too. Barefoot publishes highly illustrated books so it helps to have cultural references. You also need to know who's who in literature.' And finally? 'Flexibility – I have to do two to three jobs at the same time, and you need to be mentally flexible to do that.'

CASE STUDY

Jamie Payne, Filmmaker at Panico Media Workshop

Although Jamie Payne started out as an actor, he became interested in film while working in Poland where he was involved in a production that combined theatre performance with video projection. He then went on to do the Foundation course run at Panico Media Workshop, where he became more involved with the company. He has recently completed his first ten-minute film, *Epiphany Fish*.

Initially Jamie thought he must go to film school in order to acquire the skills he would need, but he saw an advert in *The Guardian* for the Foundation course and called them up to ask what it was all about: 'They asked me to come in, have a look round and a chat, so I went in and met the director of the course, Bob Doyle. We spoke for two hours about the pros and cons of going to film school as opposed to a short course, which is what Panico runs, especially if you're a mature student and money isn't readily available. It made sense to me because there are evening sessions, which meant I could work during the day and have instruction by top industry professionals during the evenings and weekends.'

Jamie's course, which lasted three weeks, entailed a brief introduction to 16mm film and the shooting of a short self-written film, but it didn't end there: 'I really thought that I must be a part of this, so I met the Director and a few others and they said, "What we must do is create life after the course", so they introduced a workshop where they seriously guide you to make decisions and even help you to prepare your CVs and apply for jobs. It's grown to such an extent now that there are about 250 members of the workshop and about 20 film projects going on at the moment, with really high production values and crews, which is wonderful.'

Jamie recently raised the money to complete his first professional short film, *Epiphany Fish*, which took him only two days to write but a year to complete: 'Looking back on it now, I wouldn't have written it. It involved underwater shoots and abandoned churches, which are great to write about but when it comes to filming are a logistical nightmare. The film was crewed by professionals, and the production from beginning to end involved around 50 people. Although it's been a good learning experience, I want to gain work from it. I think short films can only really exist as a calling card to a certain extent – there's a very rare chance that you actually make money from a short film. It's the features and the documentaries that you can really sell.' Jamie is currently working on a script for a new feature film while also working on other Panico productions.

Any advice?
Jamie's advice to budding filmmakers is to plunge in at the deep end and, where there is the opportunity, make a film: 'Get advice, make the film, and it's amazing the amount you'll learn because you'll have to. If you don't swim, you'll drown, and the only way to drown is if you haven't thought it out enough and the process has been rushed.'

APPLICATIONS

☐ CURRICULUM VITAE

CVs written for media jobs tend to follow a fashion, and the guidelines offered here are a result of what prospective employers have said they really do look for today.

● Be concise

All jobs in film, television, radio and publishing tend to be highly competitive, so the people responsible for reading your CV will be reading hundreds, sometimes thousands, of others. Therefore one of the first guidelines is: keep it brief and concise, or they might not even bother reading it. It is best to keep your CV to one side of A4 only. Although this may seem impossible, the personnel officer reading your CV does not want to know the intimate details of every Saturday job that you have ever done, or all the hobbies you are interested in – unless of course these hobbies are directly relevant. You will find that if you avoid narrative in writing your CV, and use key words instead, your employer is more likely to read it. It sounds more professional too. Try to ensure that you only include information in your CV that will really be of interest and leave out the irrelevant bits. Remember it must be short and have impact.

● Simply designed and easy to read

Make your CV look attractive and easy to read, but don't try to dress it up by using colours or fancy designs. These sorts of CVs, although once popular, are rarely even read these days. The exception, of course, is if you are applying for a job where you will need to demonstrate your design or computer skills.

● Employment history and work experience

After your personal details – name, address, telephone number and date of birth – you can put your qualifications or employment history. It is sometimes regarded as better to put your qualifications *after* your employment history for the simple reason that employers are largely more interested – at least initially – in your experience than your qualifications. Of course you can include your work experience under the employment history section. Any evidence that you can provide of your commitment to the industry is vital, whether it be writing for your local paper or as a volunteer runner at the National Film and Television School.

● **Qualifications**
Unless requested, it is not essential to list all the grades of your qualifications or the addresses and telephone numbers of all the schools you have ever been to. If employers are interested in you, and want to obtain references from your previous head, they can get that information from you at a later date. They are more likely, however, to be interested in contacting your university.

● **Skills and personal qualities**
If you do not have work experience to offer – you may even be applying for work experience – you can sell yourself by writing down the transferable and specialised skills that you have acquired, such as typing or editing skills, and the personal qualities that you can offer, such as efficiency and a vital sense of humour!

● **Tailoring your CV**
Don't write a standard CV and think that's it. You must always write your CV according to the job for which you are applying. A company recruiting an Assistant Researcher will be looking for different attributes from a company recruiting a Marketing Manager.

The most fundamental thing your CV should achieve is to make the interviewer want to meet you. Well-written CVs are essential in this competitive industry, not only for writing to prospective employers, but also if you are applying for a trainee scheme or work experience. You must present and market yourself professionally, so being able to put yourself across well on paper is vital.

☐ APPLYING FOR WORK OR TRAINING

The adverts

Adverts for job vacancies and training schemes in film, television, radio and publishing can be found in Monday's *Media Guardian* section or Saturday's *Guardian* careers supplement and from various national and trade magazines: *Audio Visual*, BIMA Newsletter, *The Bookseller, Broadcast, Campaign, Daily Telegraph, Evening Standard* (Wednesdays), *Independent* (Tuesdays), *Internet Magazine, Media Week, Multimedia News, Observer, PC Interactive, Printing World, Publishing News, The Radio Magazine, Screen International, Stage, Screen and Radio, Stage and Television Today, Sunday Times, Televisual, Time Out, Times, UK Press Gazette*. The BBC also advertises vacancies on CEEFAX page 696, and in its in-house magazine *Ariel*.

The criteria

Of course not all jobs are advertised. Many are filled through networking, so it is always good to keep in touch with what is going on in the industry if you can. When you do see a job vacancy or training scheme listed in the paper, check the criteria that the successful applicant must match – eg a minimum of two years' work experience in television – before you apply. If you don't fulfil the criteria the company is looking for, you will be wasting your time, because there will be plenty of other applicants applying who do. If you do match all the criteria, all well and good. Send off your CV, or request an application form if that is what you are asked to do.

Application forms

Jobs at the BBC always require you to send off, or call in, for application forms. Janet Cousins, who is responsible for the graduate trainee schemes at the BBC, says that some of the responses she had on the application forms for last year's Production Trainee Scheme were quite appalling: 'They didn't read the information properly, or fill out the form properly, or even read the advert properly. Some of the written pieces were rambling. They need to be tight and concise. The people who were shortlisted were simply those who did what was required of them, and had good realistic programme ideas – not from dreamland!' Make sure you read all the information you are given very carefully.

Research

Of course it is essential to research thoroughly the area of work that you want to go into, and if possible get some work experience before applying for a job. Working for a short period of time for free for a production or publishing company is also an excellent way of assessing if the media industry is really for you. Working long hours under pressure and in not very glamourous conditions can be a real eye opener, but at least you can leave if you want to.

☐ WORK EXPERIENCE

Work experience – working for free in return for seeing if you can stand the pressure and to add that much necessary demonstration of your commitment to the industry – is not necessarily an easy thing to get into. Today there is such high competition for jobs in the industry that many people are willing to work for free and there simply isn't the work available to match the demand. The BBC gets about a thousand requests a month for work experience, but rarely take on runners, in fact it barely offers work experience. But don't let this make you give up; there are other avenues you can try.

Once you know the area that you wish to work in, and have thoroughly researched it, write off to independent production companies or publishing houses asking for work experience opportunities, making it clear that you are prepared to work for free. It may be that out of all the letters you send, or all the phone calls you make, you are only invited in for a chat so that they may give you some advice, but this will be of great benefit to you.

Ways to get work experience

If you are interested in film or television, you could always add your name to the volunteer crew list at the National Film and Television School. If journalism or publishing is the area you want to get into, maybe you could help produce a newsletter or prospectus in the publishing department of a company or professional institution, or see if your local newspaper needs a helping hand. Hospital radio is also a potential avenue to explore. Another good way to get into the industry is via temp work. There are temping agencies that specialise in jobs with the media and publishing companies – these will be advertised in the relevant press, such as *The Guardian* on Mondays.

Most potential employers want to see clear evidence of your commitment to working in the industry, other than simply projects you may have worked on at school or college. This means practical hands-on experience. It may be that you get work as a runner, which entails making tea, sweeping floors and running errands, but it will still count in your favour as real experience of the industry as opposed to simply student productions.

Indeed, some employers may be suspicious of you if you have completed a 'media' degree, as they tend to presume these are about theorising and critical analysis as opposed to 'getting your hands dirty'. If your degree entailed practical training and/or work placements you should emphasise this on your CV. The BBC looks for students who have gained experience outside their degree programme, such as writing for their local paper or making their own programme. This shows evidence of a person's interest, initiative and motivation as well as their experience.

☐ INTERVIEWS

If you get to the interview stage, or are able to meet with a person who may be looking for someone to fill a job vacancy, you may be asked to show some samples of your work – ie to demonstrate that you really are committed to the industry. This could be in the form of a portfolio of press cuttings if it is a journalist post you are looking for. Remember, you don't only have to show pieces of work that have already been published, you may have an essay or a short story that would be of interest. Other samples of work you may like to present are showreels, a selection of well-presented photographs or a business plan.

Equally important, do your research on the company that has asked to meet you. It is essential that you know as much about the company as possible so that you can discuss the aim of the business and talk about it. Be prepared to discuss your CV (you might be asked to explain what you mean when you say you are 'well organised') and don't forget to be prepared for the most important question of all, 'Why do you think you should get the job?'

Julian Hanshaw, third-year student on the Animation course at the NFTS

After completing a Foundation course at Watford, Julian did a three-year Fine Arts degree in Wolverhampton. He then spent two years making his own small independent films before his girlfriend suggested he should apply for the postgraduate course in Animation at the National Film and Television School (NFTS). His initial reaction was that an 'ordinary Joe' like him didn't stand a chance of getting in to this prestigious school. With a bit of persuasion, however, he applied and sent in a showreel with examples of his animated work.

Julian feels he was selected for interview because he was able to demonstrate he could work off his own bat and show initiative. He began a one-week induction course, designed to weed out those students not wholly committed to the course. By the end of the week only four out of ten remained.

Each year, Julian has been able to work on three films, working within set budgets provided for by the school, starting at £1000 for the first year and rising to £7000 in his final year. Each film must have a written proposal with detailed plans of how the money is being used.

In 1997 the courses at the NFTS changed to become fee-based. When Julian entered the school, he did not have to pay. The courses now cost in the region of £3500 per year, although students are issued with a small living fee. Having said this, the Head of the School has assured Julian they are making big efforts to get sponsorship for people who want to do the courses but are unable to pay, 'So don't let the cost of the courses put anyone off'.

Julian's specialist area is drawn animation and when he graduates his work will be shown at the National Film Theatre where people from the industry will be present. It is at this event Julian hopes to network his way into the profession, either by working for a company or to do his own films. Julian is realistic in his expectations in that he knows he will probably have to do his time in the industry before being able to make his own film.

He does feel, however, that the reputation of the NFTS will aid him into getting work slightly higher up the ladder than normally would be expected of someone just entering the industry. While doing his course, Julian has also been able to work with professionals from places like the BBC, 'so they do get to know you and your work, and this does help to open the door a little bit wider'.

Julian has had his films shown publicly, at various festivals round Europe including one piece of work entitled *Holiday* at the prestigious Edinburgh Festival in 1997. His television work includes a logo sting for *Four Mations* on Channel 4.

Any advice?
'Don't be put off by the grandeur of the NFTS. Get your showreel together and don't judge it for yourself, let the school judge your potential for you. Go for it, because you have three great years to spend making your own films.'

EQUAL OPPORTUNITIES

'In terms of training at the new entrant level, there are a lot of women coming through on the trainee schemes and ethnic minorities as well... it's difficult to say categorically whether that's working through into the mainstream production. When you look around there is still an imbalance, there's no doubt about that... I think it's something we just have to keep beavering away at and accept that it's going to take time. But there have been changes in attitudes, there have been changes in approaches and I think we're getting there gradually.' Sue Davies from the ITV Network Centre

For many years sections of our society – specifically women, various ethnic groups and disabled people – have been discriminated against by the domineering group – the decision-makers, those in authority (who have tended to be male). The media industry is sadly no different, but thanks to the instigation of equal opportunities and positive action, this situation is set to improve. Equal opportunities issues are now taken seriously by the majority of employers.

This section on equal opportunities looks briefly at ways the media is responding to reflect the male/female, multicultural and multiabled society we live in today, and what the industry employers are doing to ensure better and more real representation of those people who have previously been given a raw deal.

☐ THE GENDER EQUATION

According to research carried out by Skillset on *Employment Patterns and Training Needs*, there are still substantial gender imbalances in specific job areas in the media. In addition, where work areas are predominantly female, such as Hair, Make-up, Research and Production Support, they are also the lowest paid. Various strategies have to be adopted to encourage less stereotyping of job roles. The introduction of the media NVQs is set to aid the implementation of change.

'NVQs are going to mean that it's not going to be possible for a cameraman to say to a woman, "Oh no sorry love, you can't possibly be Assistant Camera because you can't pick it up, you're not strong enough." The certificate will be there and the demonstration of the fact that they are competent to do the job will be there.' Dinah Caine from Skillset

The BBC also claims to be redressing the gender balance with a number of positive action schemes to improve the working conditions of employees. In the BBC's *The Way In: Job Opportunities In The BBC* we learn: 'a number of schemes and working arrangements have been implemented in the BBC to help people balance their careers with their personal lives. For instance there are job sharers and part-timers in all areas of the BBC'. Job sharing enables parents, and single parents who have the sole responsibility of bringing up their children (generally women) to have time to care for them while simultaneously following their career goals.

In addition, various groups have been set up, such as Women in Publishing (for those who want to get into publishing and those already established within it), to encourage the promotion of women into top management positions.

While the current situation is far from ideal, people working in the industry believe the mood is changing, or at least recognise that it does need to change.

'The industry is changing very slowly. It's certainly changed in America. I mean, in America there are a lot of female Assistant Directors and women working in the film industry at all levels. In this country it's not changing quite so quickly, but it's happening.' Natasha Ross – freelancer in the film industry

☐ ETHNIC GROUPS

The media in this country has not always given a true reflection of the multicultural society we live in today. Although the situation has improved slightly in recent years, many ethnic groups are still under-represented in the film, broadcasting, video and publishing industries.

Although these days we are more likely to see different ethnic groups presenting shows on our TV screens, or demonstrating washing-up powders in commercials, there is still a lack of diversity of ethnic origins in general on television and film, in front of and behind the camera. The same is true of radio and publishing – unless the show or magazine is aimed at particular ethnic groups, such as *Sunrise Radio* and *The Voice*. But introducing a greater cultural diversity into the mainstream media still needs to be improved.

Under-representation of certain ethnic groups may not always be a result of discrimination by the industry, but may be reinforced from cultural self-discrimination. Asian families, for example, have tended to encourage their children to follow a more secure route of employment. If we refer to Asian people being under-represented in the media, the presumption is that Asian people want to work in this industry, and research has shown us that, for cultural reasons, this may not always be the case. But the climate is definitely changing, and as Asian people are beginning to gain more information about the media and the impact it has on people's perceptions, they are beginning to accept media as a serious vocational choice; a career where the image of British Asians can be less of a stereotype, and more of a reality.

'I'm interested in working within the media because I don't think that there's a fair representation of Black and Asian people, especially women in programme-making and in film-making. So the only way to overcome what is produced on Asian and Black people is to get into the industry yourself and then do whatever you want to portray a more positive image – especially of women.'
Neila Butt, Thames Valley University

'It was non-existent a few years ago, but now you get Asian presenters in virtually every single programme, so there's no big deal about it anymore.'   Keith, an Asian Economics student

☐ DISABILITY

'In recent years, disabled people have been complaining with increasing vigour about their poor representation in film and television, and of negative images conveyed about disability. This is seen to be linked partly to the fact that few disabled people are

*employed in the film and television industry, and to the lack of
training opportunities in the sector for disabled people.*

*'Although opportunities for appearing professionally in front of
camera have increased, training in programme-making and other
technical skills is still extremely difficult to get, as is the
opportunity to 'handle' video and film in informal recreational
courses.*

*'Training opportunities at every level need to be increased if
disabled people are to develop confidence in using the medium for
themselves, whether as a craft, a tool for self-advocacy or as a
means of creative expression. A positive development is that
disabled people are now being seen as a part of general Equal
Opportunities policies within organisations.'*

(From the Focus Report – A conference looking at
Access to Training in Film and
Video for Disabled People)

Fewer than a third of disabled people are in work and this low rate
of employment is also reflected in the media industry, which could be
used as a powerful tool to support the representation and rights of
disabled people.

*'We don't have many disabled people applying. Our policy would be
to very much treat them the same as anyone else, as far as you can.
Certainly we've had, and still have, disabled people working here,
but not many disabled people apply, and I don't know why that is.'*
Katrina Ray from IPC Magazines

Why don't disabled people apply for jobs? Or do they, but get lost at
the selection stage? Do disabled people have access to the right sort
of training?

*'I'm sure we could [cater for disabled trainees] because we have
very good relationships with all the facilities companies and
equipment suppliers... but the situation hasn't arisen.'*
Anne Fenton, Skillset

Are disabled people aware of the possibilities that they have for
training? Are they targeted properly, or does information about
training only reach them when courses are run specifically for people
with disabilities?

'There haven't been many disabled people coming through trainee schemes yet, but there have been a number of one-off trainee placements specifically for disabled people which have proved very beneficial.' Sue Davies from the ITV Network Centre

Disabled people looking for either professional or non-professional training in the media may have several criteria that they would wish a potential training scheme to meet. Do the trainers have experience in working with disabled people? Are trainers aware of our needs? Is equipment accessible to disabled people?

Apart from following the usual route into journalism – by starting off with a provincial paper – disabled people may also be interested to know that RADAR, the Royal Association for Disability and Rehabilitation supplies grants for students who want to follow a career in journalism.

Although universities in general have started to address the issue of environmental access to their educational establishments, it seems few have taken the necessary steps to encourage people with disabilities on to their media courses. This problem needs to be addressed if disabled people are going to get the necessary training in order to compete in the market place.

Short courses, whether professional or non-professional, are useful as a stepping stone for gaining access either to courses of higher education or for training schemes. The 'hands-on' experience gained from short courses enables students to gauge their own level of enthusiasm and where their talents or interests lie. In addition, any steps taken to build up a CV and track record of experience is essential to gaining future work (contact Connections, address on page 69).

On a positive note, the larger employers are actively seeking to recruit disabled people, so if you are confident you can get the work done, apply for that job vacancy.

Colin Hambrook, on DAIL (Disability Arts In London) Magazine

The 'Traineeship', Colin's first post at *DAIL*, was a very open arrangement: 'It was very much about me deciding what I want to learn, and I was learning all the time, setting myself tasks.' Although Colin has always had an interest in writing on all levels, his training was in fine art: 'I always fantasised about writing for a living, but I didn't really feel journalism was an option for me because of my background – coming from a mental health system.'

When the trainee position at *DAIL* was advertised, Colin jumped at it. The post, an Arts Council initiative, was a 'good thing to find, because it gives people with disabilities access to a journalism career'. Colin did a lot of research for the job, thinking about the politics of the Disability Movement. He also had the advantage that, on and off for the previous five years, he had been involved in the Survivors Movement (the Campaign against Psychological Oppression) for which he had written poetry and other material.

Colin believes that he was selected from the seven other short-listed applicants because: 'I showed a commitment to the Disability Movement as a whole. My background helped me, as well as the enthusiasm and motivation I had to take on the traineeship post and develop it. I also had a few bits of published work that I took to the interview. And we had to write an essay as part of the remit for the interview.'

Colin was sent on four-month courses throughout the year as part of his training. The courses 'centred on the financial aspect of job-funding criteria and proposals and how to manage the books. The Arts Council seemed to think this the most important aspect. I didn't get sent on any journalism courses, because I should have already proved that I have journalism skills.'

The Traineeship lasted a year and was 'very diverse – I was out and about doing something different every day.' Since the first edition of this book, a new trainee was taken on and Colin has gone on to become the editor of *DAIL*, initially as a jobshare post, but now full time. His experience and the enormous range of skills he has developed (eg computer literacy, understanding how to subedit, ability to work to deadlines etc) contributed to his success.

Any advice?

Colin's advice to other would-be journalists is to get writing, and get work published: 'Its always an incentive to get your work in print. I found a good way to start was to write letters to papers and magazines. I got a lot of things published in the papers of the political organisations I was involved with. Even if you get work produced in a photocopied pamphlet, this is still valid and will give yourself the motivation to go on writing. People will read the pamphlet and give you feedback and tell you ways that you can improve your work, so get writing!'

SUMMARY

If having read this far, you still want to follow a career in the media and be one step ahead of the competition, consider these final points:

● Check the attributes listed at the front of this book. Consider your own skills and personality and assess whether you really are suited to a job in the media.

● Read as much as you can about the media (see Further Reading, page 66), and talk to people already working in the industry.

● Once you know what job area you really want to go into, focus yourself on achieving that goal.

● Do as much as you can to enhance your employability by gaining relevant skills through specialised short courses and degrees; get training and look into NVQs.

● Get as much work experience wherever and whenever you possibly can. Organise your own personal projects as evidence of your self-motivation and commitment.

● Write a CV that markets you effectively.

● Make and maintain contacts in the industry; write in to and call companies and follow up any response you receive.

● Keep an eye on the relevant trade journals and national media press so that you are up-to-date and knowledgeable about the industry and don't miss out on any advertised job/trainee opportunities.

● Maintain your enthusiasm – don't let rejections put you off and keep a flexible approach.

Do all of the above, be persistent, and you stand a better chance of getting in and getting on. *Good luck!*

Teresa Cross, Director and Producer of her own production company, Flying Fish

Prior to studying for a BA in Design and Media Management at Thames Valley University, Teresa Cross worked for ten years as a secretary for various media companies including Fitch Design and Virgin Group. After graduating, Teresa set up her own production company, Flying Fish.

During her final year at TVU, Teresa working with her partner of the time, Christina Clayton, producing a series of videos for the British Paralympic Association. 'We didn't realise it at the time, but it gathered momentum and it ended up with us going out to the Paralympic Games in Barcelona – after we graduated – and filming two programmes. The Sports Council then heard about us and wanted us to do some videos for them, so the work kept coming in.'

Teresa's partner decided to move on to work as a runner for LWT, but Teresa, being several years older, wasn't prepared to go and work for someone else, especially having to start at the bottom, as she suspected she would. In any case the work still kept coming in. 'Without Christina, I didn't really have an identity, so I started Flying Fish as a way of meeting the demand for the work that was coming through, I didn't sort of sit down and think I really wanted to have a production company; it just evolved.'

Since beginning at her company, Teresa has completed four projects, one for the Royal British Legion, a conference shoot for Her Majesty's Prison Service, a shoot and an edit for the Dyslexia Organisation, and another video for the Sports Council. Although Teresa is proactive in seeking work, all her work has been gained through contacts. 'I do cold calling, I write letters, I do lovely proposals and everything, but this industry is so competitive. There are so many people out there doing what I'm doing. The industry seems to be very much based on word of mouth and who you know.'

In order to set up Flying Fish, Teresa had to get a loan from the bank. It was here that the business side of the DAMM degree really paid off: 'I presented them with a business plan that I drew up myself and they were really impressed.'

Finally, how did Christina Clayton get a job as a runner for LWT? Teresa says: 'She heard about this job as a runner going at LWT via a friend of her mothers, so she called up and hassled this guy morning, noon and night for an interview. It was for a job as a technical runner in the edit suites, and she had no electronics background or anything. She just knew a bit of the jargon from what we had done, and she was up against six other guys. She got the job.

'That was really good going, wasn't it? She started off on £7000 and was really making tea and coffee, but she was very aggressive in letting people know what she wanted to do. Sure enough she's got on really well and she's earning good money now as a Programme Assistant for the *London Programme*.'

DIRECTORY

Further reading

Careers in... series, published by Kogan Page, includes the titles: *Careers in Publishing, Careers in Journalism, Careers in Film and Video, Careers in Television and Radio*

Getting into Broadcasting by Fiona Russell, Trotman

Lights Camera Action: Careers in Film, Television and Video by Josephine Langham, BFI Publications

GET (Graduate Employment and Training), Gives details on journalism and other related courses, eg communication skills, media, publishing and graphic design. CRAC–Hobsons

Get Tuned In produced by Chris Davies. Three videos funded by the Employers Forum on Disability of which the Broadcasters Forum is a subgroup

Listing of Short Courses in Media and Multimedia, BFI Publications.

Media Courses UK edited by Lavinia Orton, BFI publications

TV News: Building a Career in Broadcast Journalism by Ray White, Focal Press

Most of the above books, and many more to do with the media, are available from Trotman. For a catalogue, Tel: 01797 369961.

Directories and handbooks

(available from most reference libraries)

The Media Guide edited by Paul Fisher and Steve Peak, Fourth Estate Ltd. Packed with a wealth of up-to-date information about the media industry

BFI Film and Television Handbook, BFI Publications. Awards, bookshops, cable and satellite, courses, facilities, festivals, funding, libraries, organisations, PR companies, press contacts, production companies, studios, TV companies (see Organisations on the next page)

Broadcasting Production Guide, EMAP Media 0171 505 8000

Creative Handbook, Variety Media Publications, 0171 637 3663

Kemps International Film, Television and Video Yearbook, Variety Media Publications

PACT: Directory of British Film and Television Producers. Company profiles, production categories and phone numbers, personnel, PACT membership contact list, international (see Organisations on the next page).

Radio Academy Yearbook (see Organisations on the next page)

66

Writers Handbook, edited by Barry Turner, Macmillan. The complete
reference for all writers and those involved in the media.

Periodicals

Black Film Bulletin, BFI Publications
Bookseller, J Whitaker and Sons
Broadcast Trade paper to keep you up to date with television and radio
industry news. An EMAP Business Publication
DAIL (Disability Arts in London) Run and staffed by people with
disabilities. Call 0171 916 6351
Television, the Royal Television Society (see Organisations below)
UK Press Gazette, Quantum

What to send off for

Association of Graduate Careers Advisory Services (AGCAS)
publishes a list of Careers Information booklets including ones on
Journalism and Writing, Publishing, Business and Information
Management and Social Research. It also publishes a booklet entitled *Job
Seeking After Graduation* which gives helpful information on matters such
as constructing your CV and how to prepare for interviews. Contact
Information Booklets, CSU, Armstrong House, Oxford Road, Manchester
M1 7ED for a list of the current order form. Tel: 0161 277 5200

Education, Training and Working in Film, Television and Broadcasting
edited by Anne Fenton and published by the Moving Image Society (see
Organisations below)
Skillset Careers Information Pack. Guidance for potential recruits to the
industry; advice on training and education and contact names and
addresses (see Organisations below)
Way In: Job Opportunities in the BBC – available from BBC Corporate
Recruitment Services, 0171 580 4468
Talent 2000. Available from BBC Education Information, 0171 746 1111

Organisations

AFVPA The Advertising Film and Video Producers' Association, 26 Noel
Street, London W1V 3RD. Tel: 0171 434 2651
BECTU Broadcasting Entertainment Cinematograph Theatre's Union,111
Wardour Street, London W1V 4AY. Tel: 0171 437 8506
BFI British Film Institute Holds conferences on the broadcast and film
industry as well as running courses and providing research facilities, 21
Stephen Street, London W1P 2LN. Tel: 0171 255 1444
BIMA British Interactive Multimedia Association, 6 Washingley Road,
Peterborough Cambs PE7 3SY. Tel: 0171 436 8250
Broadcast Journalism Training Council, The Coach House, West
Bridgeford, Notts NG2 7NH. Tel: 0171 727 9522

The Moving Image Society – BKSTS 63–71 Victoria House, Vernon Place, London WC1B 4DA. Tel: 0171 242 8400. Produces an updated list of training for newcomers as well as running training courses itself. There is student membership for those wishing to make industry contacts – £22.50 per annum. It also runs a Film Foundation Course for students at only £85 plus VAT.

NCTJ National Council for the Training of Journalists, Latton Bush Centre, Southern Way, Harlow, Essex, CM18 7BL; 01279 430009

Networking: The Film, Video and Television Organisation for Women Vera Productions, 30–38 Dock Street, Leeds LS10 1JF. Tel: 0113 242 8646A quarterly newsletter, entry in the NETWORKING index, advice and help and a campaigning voice. Welcomes anyone involved or interested in film, video, television and the media.

Newspaper Society Bloomsbury House, Bloomsbury Square, 74–77 Great Russell Street, London WC1B 3DA; 0171 636 7014

NUJ National Union of Journalists, Acorn House, 314–320 Grays Inn Road, London WC1X 8DP; 0171 278 7916

PACT Producers' Alliance for Cinema and Television. PACT has a Getting Started course for new and aspiring producers who are members of PACT 45 Mortimer Street, London W1N 7TD; 171 331 6000

Panico Media Workshop Panico Studio, 1 Falconberg Court, London W1V5FG 0171 734 5120

PPA Periodicals Publishers' Association, Queens House, 28 Kingsway, London WC2B 6JR; 0171 404 4166

RADAR Royal Association for Disability and Rehabilitation, 12 City Forum, 250 City Road, London EC1V 8HF

Radio Academy PO Box 4SZ, London W1A 4SZ; 0171 255 2010

Royal Television Society 100 Gray's Inn Road, London WC1X 8AL. Tel: 0171 430 1000. Student membership available; courses and seminars

Skill: National Bureau for Students with Disabilities 336 Brixton Road, London SW9 7AA. Tel: 0171 274 0565; Information Service 0171 978 9890

Skillset The industry training organisation for broadcast, film and video. 2nd Floor, 91–101 Oxford Street, London W1R 1RA. Tel: 0171 534 5300

Society of Young Publishers 12 Dyott Street, London WC1A 1DF. Tel: 0181 551 3974

Women in Film and Television Garden Studios, 11–15 Betterton Street, London WC2H 9BP; 0171 379 0344

Useful addresses

Arts Council of England, 14 Great Peter Street, London SW1P 3NQ. Tel: 0171 333 0100

Arts Council of Wales, Holst House, Museum Place, Cardiff CF1 3NX. Tel: 01633 875075

BBC Corporate Recruitment Services, PO Box 7000, London W12 7ZY. Tel: 0171 580 4468

BSkyB, 6 Centaurs Business Park, Grant Way, Isleworth, Middlesex, TW7 7QD. Tel: 0171 705 3000
British Interactive Broadcasting, 47–53 Canon Street, London, EC4H 5SQ. Tel: 0171 489 7770
Channel 4, 124 Horseferry Road, London, SW1P 2TX. Tel: 0171 396 4444
Channel 5, Duty Office, PO Box 55, Nottingham, NG1 5HE. Tel: 0345 050505
Chapterhouse, 2 Southernhay West, Exeter, Devon EX1 1JG. Tel: 01935 816262
Connections Communications Centre, Palingswick House, 241 King Street, London, W6 9LP. Tel: 0181 741 1766
Department of Culture, Media and Sport 2–4 Cockspur Street SW1Y 5DH. Tel: 0171 211 6266
FT2: Film and Television, Freelance Training, 4th Floor, Warwick House, 9 Warwick Street, London W1R 5RA. Tel: 0171 734 5141
Independent Television Network, Centre 200 Gray's Inn Road, London WC1X 8HF. Tel: 0171 843 8000
London Arts Board, Elme House, 133 Long Acre, Covent Garden, WC2E 9AF. Tel: 0171 240 1313
London College of Printing, Elephant and Castle, London SE1 6SB. Tel: 0171 514 6569
London School of Publishing, 69 Notting Hill Gate, London W11 3JS. Tel: 0171 221 3399
Media Production Facilities, Bon Marche Building, Ferndale Road, London SW9 8EJ. Tel: 0171 737 7152
National Film and Television School, Beaconsfield Studios, Station Road, Beaconsfield, Bucks HP9 1LG. Tel: 01494 671234
PMA Training PMA House, 3 Church Passage, St Ives, Cambridgeshire PE17 4AY. Tel: 01480 300653
Publishing Training Centre, Book House, 45 East Hill, Wandsworth, London SE18 2QZ. Tel: 0181 874 2718
Publishers Association, 1 King's Way, London WC2 6XF. Tel: 0171 565 7474
Reuters, 85 Fleet Street, London, EC4P 4AJ. Tel: 0171 250 1122
Scottish Arts Council, 12 Manor Place, Edinburgh EH3 7DD. Tel: 0131 226 6051
The Sheffield College, Norton Centre, Dyche Lane, Sheffield S8 8BR. Tel: 0114 260 2600
Thames Valley University, St Mary's Road, Ealing, London W5 5RF. Tel: 0181 579 5000

Publishers

BFI Publications (see Organisations, page 67)
CRAC–Hobsons, Bateman Street, Cambridge CB2 1LZ. Tel: 01223 460277
DAIL, 34 Osnaburgh Street, London NW1 3ND. Tel: 0171 916 6351
EMAP Media, 33–39 Bowling Green Lane, London EC1R 0DA. Tel: 0171 505 8000

Focal Press, Linacre House, Jordan Hill, Oxford OX2 8DP. Tel: 01865 310366
Fourth Estate Ltd, 6 Salem Road, London W2 4BU. Tel: 0171 727 8993
Kogan Page, 120 Pentonville Road, London N1. Tel: 0171 278 0433
Macmillan, 25 Eccleston Place, London SW1W 9NA. Tel: 0171 881 8000
PACT (see Organisations on page 68)
Quantum, 19 Scarbrook Road, Croydon, Surrey CR9 1LX. Tel: 0181 565 4448
Trotman and Co Ltd, 12 Hill Rise, Richmond, Surrey TW10 6UA. Tel: 0181 940 5668. Book orders 01797 369961
Variety Media Publications, 34–35 Newman Street, London W1P 3PD. Tel: 0171 637 3663
J Whitaker & Sons, 12 Dyott Street, London WC1A 1DF. Tel: 0171 420 6000